SMOKE

SMOKE

Confessions of a Cuban Cigar Smuggler

SCOTT ANTHONY

COPYRIGHT © 2026 SCOTT ANTHONY MEDIA LLC
All rights reserved.

SMOKE
Confessions of a Cuban Cigar Smuggler

FIRST EDITION

ISBN   978-1-5445-5069-5 *Hardcover*
          978-1-5445-5068-8 *Paperback*
          978-1-5445-5070-1 *Ebook*

In Loving Memory of Howard Frum, "The Rolex King"

Howard was more than the Rolex King. He was a fixture in his shop, a fixer who knew everyone, a man who loved the buzz of people coming and going all day long. He lit up the room with stories, laughter, and magic tricks—especially for kids. Just two months before his passing, I stood in that shop with my daughter and he amazed her with tricks and even gave her a watch she treasures.

Howard was also the first person I ever brought my Cuban cigars to. I showed up unannounced with suitcases full, and, without hesitation, he picked up the phone and began calling his network. By the end of my smuggling years, nearly every customer I had was because of him.

I wanted nothing more than to hand Howard the first copy of this book. I can see him now, holding it up, walking around his store, showing everyone: "Look at this—here I am. This is my friend." That was Howard—proud, loud, and larger than life.

This book is for him.

This book is for you, Howard.

CONTENTS

PREFACE 9
1. WELCOME TO REALITY 13
2. A BUYER'S GUIDE TO CUBA 25
3. FIRST RUN—ALL OR NOTHING 39
4. UNDERSTANDING CIGARS 59
5. MCALLEN 79
6. HARD LABOR 95
7. THE COST OF DOING BUSINESS 105
8. BUSTED 137
9. THE BEGINNING OF FACTORY CIGARS 155
10. THE CIGAR GUY 171
11. FAKES 183
12. THE BOYS 197
13. GOOD FELLA 213
14. POOR ANDERSON 223
15. THE WRITING IS ON THE WALL 237
    ACKNOWLEDGMENTS 253
    ABOUT THE AUTHOR 257

PREFACE
FORBIDDEN LUXURY

IN EARLY FEBRUARY 1962, JUST HOURS BEFORE SIGNING THE US trade embargo on Cuba, President John F. Kennedy had one last piece of business—personal business. He called in his press secretary, Pierre Salinger, and gave him a very specific assignment: get me every Cuban cigar you can find, and do it before morning. Salinger combed Washington like a man on a mission and came back with about 1,200 of Kennedy's favorite H. Upmanns. The next day, with his stash safely tucked away, Kennedy put pen to paper and signed the order that cut off Cuban imports for decades.

The embargo was born from the ashes of the Cuban Revolution. In 1959, Fidel Castro overthrew the corrupt Batista regime, aligning Cuba with the Soviet Union in the throes of the Cold War. Tension between the US and Cuba escalated rapidly. Castro's nationalization of American businesses and the Bay of Pigs fiasco in 1961 drove Kennedy to cut off diplomatic ties. The embargo, formalized through the

Foreign Assistance Act of 1961 and expanded in 1962, economically isolated Cuba and undermined Castro's government.

But for cigar aficionados, the embargo wasn't just a geopolitical maneuver—it was sacrilege. Cuba, long regarded as the Mecca of cigar craftsmanship, had cultivated a mystique around its tobacco. Its fertile Pinar del Río region produced the finest leaves, rolled by *torcedores* whose skills bordered on artistry. To Americans, Cuban cigars were more than a luxury; they were an emblem of status, power, and indulgence.

The embargo gutted the legal trade in Cuban cigars overnight. Retailers scrambled to clear their inventories, and aficionados hoarded their stashes like wartime rations. The void left by Cuban cigars created opportunities for other producers to enter the market—notably in the Dominican Republic, Nicaragua, and Honduras. These countries adopted Cuban seeds and emulated traditional techniques, giving rise to a "New World" cigar industry. While these cigars gained respectability, purists derided them as imitations, forever chasing the unattainable allure of the Cuban puro.

Meanwhile, Cuba capitalized on its newfound exclusivity. The state-run cigar monopoly, Cubatabaco, turned Cuban cigars into a symbol of defiance against American imperialism. To own or smoke a Cuban cigar became a subtle act of rebellion, an unspoken nod to forbidden pleasures.

As demand for Cuban cigars persisted, the embargo unintentionally birthed a thriving black market. Smugglers, middlemen, and counterfeiters entered the fray, creating a shadow economy that stretched from Havana's factories to the private humidors of Wall Street executives. Cuban cigars became contraband, their scarcity and illegality only enhancing their cachet.

The mechanics of smuggling were as varied as the players involved. Some traffickers operated on a small scale, slipping boxes of cigars into their luggage on return flights from Canada, Mexico, or Europe—countries unaffected by the embargo. Others orchestrated elaborate operations involving fishing boats, shipping containers, and diplomatic pouches. Fake labels and counterfeit cigars flooded the market, blurring the line between authenticity and forgery.

Inevitably, organized crime took notice. The profitability of smuggling Cuban cigars attracted the same criminal networks that trafficked in drugs and weapons. In the 1980s and '90s, cigar smuggling operations grew increasingly sophisticated. Miami became a hub for illicit activity, with shipments often passing through the city's labyrinthine ports and warehouses. Distributors forged connections with Cuban insiders, bribing factory workers and customs officials to ensure a steady supply.

Among the most notorious cases was Operation Smoke Ring, a multi-agency investigation in 1996–1997 led by the US Customs Service with partner agencies including the US Postal Inspection Service, the Miami–Dade Police Department, and the Florida State Attorney's Office. The operation uncovered a network moving thousands of genuine Cuban cigars from Central America into the United States and resulted in arrests and prosecutions under the Trading With the Enemy Act and 18 U.S.C. § 545.

One of the best-known prosecutions from that era was *United States v. Richard M. Connors* (N.D. Ill.). Connors, a Chicago attorney, was convicted in 2002 of smuggling Cuban cigars through Central America, with related counts including conspiracy, smuggling, and violations of the Trading with the Enemy Act; he was sentenced in 2004.

In New York, a coordinated August 1998 crackdown targeted Manhattan clubs and restaurants found selling Cuban cigars in violation of the Trading with the Enemy Act. Raids included the Racquet & Tennis Club and Patroon Restaurant and led to the arrests of managers and several buyers.

THE LEGACY OF THE EMBARGO

Despite—or perhaps because of—the embargo, Cuban cigars achieved an almost mythical status in American culture. They appeared in films, music, and literature as symbols of indulgence and rebellion. From Tony Montana's ever-present cigar in *Scarface* to the celebratory smokes of Wall Street bankers, Cuban cigars became synonymous with the good life, even as their legal acquisition remained illegal.

The mystique also fueled an underground community of aficionados. Private cigar clubs and "speakeasies" catered to those willing to pay a premium for authentic Cuban smokes. Collectors traded boxes of cigars like rare artifacts, complete with provenance records and meticulous storage conditions. For these devotees, the risk of prosecution paled in comparison to the joy of lighting up a perfectly rolled fine Cuban cigar.

The Cuban embargo has endured for over six decades, surviving countless debates, reforms, and presidential administrations. While its effectiveness as a geopolitical strategy remains contested, its impact on the cigar industry is undeniable. It created an ecosystem of innovation, counterfeiting, and smuggling that reshaped the global cigar market.

Today, Cuban cigars are still contraband in the United States, though relaxed travel restrictions during the Obama administration briefly allowed Americans to bring back small quantities for personal use. Even so, the black market persists, its roots too deep to be eradicated by policy shifts alone.

This book delves into the clandestine world of Cuban cigar smuggling during the 1990s, a decade when the cigar craze in the US reached a fever pitch. It's a story of risk and reward, of shadowy deals and sunlit beaches adorned with ever-willing beautiful women, of meticulous craftsmanship, and brazen criminality. It's a story about a man with a dream and unyielding persistence who defied borders, laws, and morality to bring a taste of forbidden luxury to those who craved it and were willing to pay handsomely to enjoy it.

As you turn these pages, consider the irony: a simple product of soil, sun, and skill became a symbol of defiance and desire, its journey from Cuba to America a testament to human ingenuity and the enduring allure of the forbidden. Welcome to the smoke-filled rooms where history, crime, and hedonism collide.

Chapter One

WELCOME TO REALITY

I DIDN'T KNOW WE WERE POOR UNTIL I WAS FOURTEEN.

Before that, I never gave it much thought. Most of the people around me lived the same way, or maybe I just didn't understand how bad it really was.

There's a video I once saw of young people on a football field. They were told to line up and take two steps forward for each statement that applied to them: "Your parents are still married," "You never had to worry about your next meal," "You had a private tutor." As I watched, I realized my truth. Some of the group moved forward fast, others stayed somewhere in the middle. Me? I would've been in dead last, standing where I started.

My father left when I was four. My mother worked whatever minimum-wage job she could get, and my grandfather—the only male figure in my life—died when I was seven. By the time I was eight, both grandparents were gone. That's when I basically hit the streets full-time.

I had no older brother, no father, and no real guidance. My mother loved me, but she had no idea how to raise a boy, especially one like me. I still remember the day she came home from a food bank with a box of supplies—powdered milk, a block of cheese, and some canned goods. I was excited, unpacking and playing with the "goodies." Then I saw her drop to her knees and start crying.

We didn't have a car. We didn't have air conditioning in the sweltering Chicago summers. We barely had enough heat in the winter. I skipped school so often that I could barely read or write. When I did go, I was usually in trouble—fighting, hustling, or just not giving a damn. Eventually, I got sent to schools for troubled youth, but I got expelled from all of them. They weren't in my neighborhood, either, which made getting there dangerous—crossing into another gang's territory could get you killed.

By nine, I had already been arrested—my first bust was for stealing a CB radio out of a car. I was in a street gang, had my first tattoo at ten, and I smoked cigarettes and drank soon after. Weed followed, then harder drugs. I became good at daytime burglaries—most people weren't home during the day, so it was easy.

I saw my first killing at thirteen. It happened during a rumble with a rival gang. I watched an older guy I knew stab another kid to death with my sword cane. I'd already seen people shooting dope in front of me since I was twelve. This was normal life in my world.

We were all kids from the wrong side of the tracks, each with our own bad-luck story. My best friend, Kevin, accidentally shot himself in the head with a .38 when he was thirteen. He was DOA at the hospital. This affected me profoundly. I was too young and ignorant to understand, but there was deep damage. He had been one of my closest friends since I was born.

My first girlfriend got pregnant when she was thirteen, and I was only twelve. She hated me for it and stalked me for years. I didn't understand any of this at the time.

By fourteen, I was leading a major section of a Chicago street gang. We were armed with baseball bats, chains, brass knuckles, knives, and even a few guns. We fought daily—sometimes more than once a day. I was all in on street life.

When my mother moved us to a suburb, I was a fish out of water. I walked differently, dressed differently, and spoke in street slang. I was a greaser in a world of preps and jocks. Somehow, I adapted and taught myself enough to graduate from a good high school, but after that, I was stuck. No one guided me toward college or a career. I was alone again. And the streets were calling.

I dove headfirst into organized crime. It came naturally to me. At seventeen, I robbed my first drug dealer—a big score that set me on a new path. The money came fast, and I spent it just as fast. I had cars, clothes, and women. I built a crew of tight, loyal friends, and we ran our neighborhood like we owned it. Over the next five years, I robbed thirty-two drug dealers at gunpoint, kicked in doors, and took what I wanted. I thought I had the world by the balls.

My fall started in 1984, after a massive shootout with Chicago police following a drug deal gone bad. The heat was on—feds, local cops, everyone was looking at me. I managed to keep going until early 1987, when I was busted on a multi-kilo run from Miami. I became a fugitive that year. Cut all ties. Went on the run. Ended up in Mexico. Years later, my wife made a comment that stuck with me. She said most young men today are soft—"pussies," in her words.

I told her about the Spartans, how they took boys from their mothers at age seven and sent them to warrior training. She said, "That's what happened to you. When your grandfather died at seven, the streets took you. That was your warrior training for the life you were going to face." She was right. That's who I am. That's the road I traveled before I ever smuggled my first Cuban cigar. And if you want to understand how I built a million-dollar underground cigar empire, you have to understand the warrior the streets made first.

I have a saying:

I DIDN'T GROW UP WITH ROLE MODELS. I JUST GREW UP AROUND PEOPLE I KNEW I DIDN'T WANT TO BE LIKE.

A WAKE-UP CALL

The real world was a foreign place to me—like another planet. The suburbs were especially alien. Until this day, I really didn't know my place in the social hierarchy.

I had met a guy named Phil who had a really pretty sister, Becky. I went to their house in Evanston, a suburb just outside of Chicago, where I was living at the time. I asked for Phil, but I was hoping to see Becky. I was invited inside and waited with his two little sisters, maybe eight and ten years old.

After just a few minutes talking to them, I realized they were already smarter and more educated than me. They knew about stuff I had no clue about—countries around the world, continents, current events. Real things. The good thing was, they were young and innocent enough not to know that I was basically a caveman. I wasn't publicly shamed, but inside I was dying. I knew the truth, and it cut deep: I was just a street kid from the other side of the tracks—the ugly, poor, gray side.

This wasn't a trivial moment. This was a revelation.

It was a wake-up call.

I was fourteen, and right then and there, I realized I didn't want to grow up to be stupid. I knew it was time to get my shit together. I needed to go back to school.

It didn't happen overnight. Bad habits die hard. I got arrested, taken before a judge, and remanded to the state—still a full-blown juvenile delinquent. But once again, I had the hand of God on my shoulder. I pleaded with the court to give me one more chance. I told them about the encounter with those two little girls and the realization that followed. I told them I didn't want to grow up to be uneducated. They listened.

They gave me one last shot. It was a Friday. If I didn't show up to school the following Monday, a warrant would be issued, and they'd lock me up and throw away the key.

From that point forward, I forced myself to study. I started educating myself. And again, the hand of God—or something—was on me. This time, in the form of Mike Lindenmayer. He was a few years older and had tried for a long time to help me go straight. For months, he showed up at my house every day until I got used to waking up on my own. A saint sent to rescue me, maybe?

On my first day back at school, I saw a woman—I didn't know who she was at the time, but she was everything I wasn't. She was gorgeous, educated, sophisticated, and well-dressed. A real woman. Way out of my league. I wasn't fooling myself. But right then, I had a reason to raise the bar.

She was probably my saving grace. She was God-sent—I have no doubt. She was the single biggest positive influence in my entire life. If not for her, I may not have evolved.

She helped guide me through many hardships and became my light. She showed me the importance of eating well—healthy, nutritious food. She inspired me to work out—not just fight, but build real muscle and endurance. She was my first introduction to a better class of people.

She gave me my first taste of self-worth. My first sense of dignity. My first glimpse of a better future.

She showed me what could be, and I'll never forget that.

Through her, I got a glimpse of a life I didn't even know existed. She introduced me to real men—not street thugs—but men who owned companies, had careers, built things. I didn't know anything like that. Sure, I had some family who were decent, middle-class people, but they lived in other areas. We were stuck in the inner city.

In the streets, you build a sixth sense for survival—at least I did.

And I dreamed of another life. A better life. But where do you start? How do you even get out? I was a street kid, no father, surrounded by a bunch of guys just like me—with a born-to-lose tattoo on our souls. Street gangs and criminal activity, that's all I really knew.

Despite all the violence, I had a network of friends and allies in other gangs. Our lives back then were perfectly captured in two movies. If you've ever seen *The Warriors*, that was us—twenty-four hours a day. Constant tension, constant motion. By fourteen, I'd already been arrested at least forty times. All the cops in my neighborhood knew my name.

The other movie was *Bad Boys* with Sean Penn—filmed in Chicago. That one hit too.

But there was one thing that really stayed with me. I used to play one song on repeat: "In the City" by Joe Walsh—the one from the end of *The Warriors*. That song was my life. It nailed the feeling of growing up on the streets—no hope, no way out, no one coming to save you.

Joe Walsh put into music what a thousand of us were living and dying through in silence.

If you've never heard it, go listen. It's not just a song—it's a survival story with a guitar behind it.

I was far from lazy. I always worked. I had many jobs, and even as a kid, I always held my own. I didn't fuck off. You could count on me. I was never fired—not once in my life. I wasn't that kind of fuck-up.

I washed dishes, delivered newspapers, did construction, painted houses, washed cars, shoveled snow in the winter, and cut grass in the summer. I worked as a clerk in an office building and packed bags, stocked shelves, and cleaned floors at a big grocery store chain. I never complained.

But here's the truth: you will never get ahead in life just being a "worker," a laborer.

You must educate yourself and work your ass off.

I have no doubt I was being watched—protected—by a force greater than myself.

God, maybe. An angel. A spirit.

Something kept me alive. I should be dead.

I faced death—or life in prison—more times than I can count. And I'm sure there are plenty of times I never even knew about.

THE TRUTH

By the time I was twenty-three, I had the DEA, ATF, FBI, Secret Service, US Marshals, and even Interpol looking for me. I had been a very bad boy. I was moving serious weight—trafficking drugs from Miami to Chicago—and running guns of every kind. There were multiple federal investigations into me for narcotics, counterfeit currency, and weapons violations.

In Chicago, I had built an organized crew of ex–gang members I'd known since we were kids. We were hitting scores: armored cars, jewelry stores, rival drug dealers. Some said we owned our neighborhoods back then. We had the nicest cars, the baddest women, and pockets stuffed with cash. For a bunch of kids from the wrong side of the tracks, this was making it.

But everything came to a screeching halt in early 1987. I got pulled over on a highway in Georgia, heading back from Miami. The truck was loaded with cocaine. I ran, and I got away. I spent three hard days running through the woods. Luckily, I'd always kept myself in top shape. I made it back to Chicago, but the air had changed. The heat was real now. I could feel it. I knew I had to leave.

My childhood friend, and one of the only people I completely trusted, David Bonomo, was sitting in a cell in Peach County Jail. I was now officially a fugitive from justice. David stayed locked up for about six months before his father got him out on bond. He took many falls for me and never once gave up. David Bonomo is a stud, a real gangster, who took many beatings from cops and never snitched.

I got his lawyer's number and called him. I asked, "If you could give Scott any advice, what would it be?"

He said, "Scott should stay in hiding for five years. That's how long it will take for David's case to be dropped. If Scott can avoid being caught, he'll have a much better chance too."

And I did it. I stayed hidden for five years.

Mexico became my target. But I made one mistake: I told a couple of guys in my crew. In the streets, it's every man for himself, and they betrayed me, hard. I felt homeless. I couldn't stay around. I had no choice. I would get caught sooner or later, or I could leave for Mexico. So I went.

My life, at fifteen, improved with just a few new habits: eating healthy and lifting weights. I worked out all the time: running, biking, boxing, and martial arts. I didn't waste my time like other guys my age. I was about working out, money, and women—in that order. I had a job but no real understanding of money or the real world. Bodybuilding and fitness became part of my identity. I was muscular, ripped, and solid. I was already studying nutrition and eating healthy.

Can you call it a dream? Maybe. I could definitely make it sound like a dream when I talked about it with passion and enthusiasm. At the very least, it was something positive to talk about.

I dreamed about owning a gym ever since I was around sixteen. Back then, in the mid-1970s, there was always that same ad in the back of bodybuilding magazines—"Own your own gym." I must have stared at that ad a hundred times. It was basic, bare bones, and nothing like the polished health clubs we see today. The ad said it cost $11,000 to get started.

I used to sit and daydream. Plan. Visualize every detail.

I started saving, working my ass off, hustling, stealing, and doing whatever I had to do to put money away. When I finally had the cash together, I bought the latest copy of the magazine…and the price had jumped to $30,000 to own a gym. Such is life. I didn't have any significant income and had no real idea what was involved with owning a business, but I could still daydream.

I was determined. I wasn't just going to open a gym; I was going to build the best. One that blended everything I loved: weightlifting, boxing, mixed martial arts, all under one roof. It was something no one had done yet.

Sometimes dreams do come true. Looking back, it seems like all the stars lined up for me. I refuse to accept that all the special people who crossed my path and helped me, along with all the good fortune, were just a coincidence. I can't accept that. It was more.

I was on the run, down and out, empty and shallow, without direction or purpose. Then the opportunity landed in front of me: a gym for sale.

Love at first sight. I fell for it like a fool in love.

In 1988, I opened my first gym. It immediately became my purpose in life. It swallowed me whole. It was the only thing on my mind, day and night. It might as well have been my destiny. I poured my heart and soul into it. It was big, not great, but it was mine.

I'd spent most of my liquid cash to make it happen, but I owned the building, three floors, 3,000 square feet, plus an adjoining 1,300-square-foot lot. As soon as I walked up the stairs to the roof, I had a vision: *I'm going to build a badass apartment up here.*

And I did. I saw it and made it happen.

I also built on the vacant lot, adding four full floors, another 5,200 square feet. It drained my savings. I poured everything into it. And when it was done, I didn't have much left in the bank. But I still had big plans, and big plans needed money.

Although I had my own gym, it wasn't enough for me. I was ambitious. I wanted more. I had already mixed weights with boxing and martial arts, like I'd always imagined. But it was still small. I wanted large. I didn't know how yet, but the want and desire were there.

While I worked my ass off and built my business brick by brick, I had a few friends in Mexico who traveled to Cuba in 1990. I wanted to go but didn't want to risk applying for a passport under another name. I had all the fake paperwork and could have made it work, but it was a big risk. It wouldn't be the smartest thing I could do. So I passed.

When they returned, they told amazing stories. I could only visualize it as they spoke. My mind floated with the dream.

I was jealous. I wished I didn't have my legal problems hanging over me. They told me about the beautiful women everywhere and how easy it was to meet them. They were cut off from the rest of the world, hungry for more than just food. Cuba had recently lost the Soviet Union's financial aid, and people were struggling. For now, all I could do was dream about going someday.

It was early January 1992 when I was finally tracked down and caught. I had been on the run for five years. Back in the day, they called it "being on the lam." It might sound exciting, but in reality, it's hard, very hard. It's not for everyone, and it doesn't usually last long for stupid people.

I lasted my five years, which was the goal David's lawyer had set. But I was tired. I was using aliases, always looking over my shoulder. I hadn't seen my family. Friends were even rarer. If you want to last on the run, you have to cut all ties. It's cold and lonely.

I was finally caught and extradited to the USA. What a ride. I was transferred from one jail to another every day for about three weeks before landing in Georgia, just over the five-year mark I'd needed.

MR. GARWOOD

I know how this might sound, and anyone can laugh if they want, but the second I saw him, something shifted inside me. He looked like the male version of my paternal grandmother—the spitting image. Her twin brother. White, white skin. Bright, piercing blue eyes. Pale blond-white hair.

That resemblance hit me hard. And instantly, I felt something I hadn't felt in weeks: peace.

Like I had just stepped into the hands of something divine. I don't care what anyone calls it—fate, destiny, God, guardian angel—it was real. In that moment, I knew I was in good hands. He was my attorney, a real attorney, honest and caring, as old-school as they come.

We built a friendship based on trust and mutual respect. He believed in me, even when he didn't have to. Even when I didn't fully believe in myself yet.

That belief, and that care, changed me.

Sitting in that Georgia jail, shackled and surrounded by chaos, I made a vow to myself: I was never going to get arrested again. I was done being a criminal. Not because the law scared me. Not because I found God in a cell. But because I had disappointed enough people in my life already.

And now here was this man, this quiet, steady Southern gentleman, who had no reason to take a chance on me. No reason to go above and beyond.

But he did.

He treated me like family. He steadied me when I was falling apart. He didn't just fight for me in court; he fought for my dignity.

I never told him. Never made some dramatic promise. But from that day forward, anytime I got close to slipping back...anytime I even thought about doing something that would risk my freedom again...I remembered Mr. Garwood.

And in his honor, I couldn't do it. I wouldn't do it.

I owed that man my future.

Fast-forward eighteen months, and I'm back on the streets—almost free. I was on for eight years of federal paper, checking in every five or six weeks. The federal court gave me blanket travel because my business and life were outside the USA.

While I had been hiding from all three-lettered government agencies, I had also been working my ass off. Unlike most criminals, I had a great work ethic. I'd become very conscious of money and worked hard to control and limit my spending. I had built a solid business—a real business that made money. I wasn't breaking any world records, but it was honest.

I was free. For the first time in seven years, I could be myself again. No more running. No more lying. No more fake names.

Once I returned to my life in Mexico, I immediately remodeled my business. I didn't just want a gym; I wanted the best gym.

I kept building. I was training and managing fighters, which I loved, but it wasn't the road to the best gym. I also brought Mexican boxing gear back to the USA on my return trips. It covered my travel expenses and made me a few bucks. Not really a business; it was just a hustle. And I hated it. Dealing with fighters and trainers isn't easy.

I had to think of something else, but I was low on ideas. Crime was always knocking at my door. That's what I knew. It followed me. But I fought back.

There were always those two devils on my left shoulder and just one angel on my right. My heart challenge was always at war. The devils talked sweet. The angel pleaded.

I had promised myself I'd never go back to street life. It wasn't easy. I'd spent most of my life in it. But I had also made that promise for Mr. Garwood. And that was one I could never break.

Chapter Two

A BUYER'S GUIDE TO CUBA

BEFORE I GET INTO MY STORY, YOU NEED TO KNOW SOMETHING about Cuba and about Cuban cigars. By the 1990s, Cuba had been under an embargo for more than thirty years, and both Cuban cigars and Cuba itself had become myths. I was about to find out the reality for myself, and make it pay for my dream life.

FIRST TRIP TO CUBA

A couple of friends and I organized a trip to Havana, Cuba, around 1994. We had booked a rental car and suites at the Marina Hemingway. I was excited at the thought of going to Havana. I knew it would be amazing.

We landed in Cuba about 2:00 p.m. It was like going back in time. It was strange. The people were dressed like the fifties and seventies, and the cars were either very old or new. I saw Russian cars, trucks, and motorcycles for the first time. I didn't know much about them, but they looked like they weren't very good quality.

Arriving in Cuba for me was surreal. I soaked it all in like a child at a toy store for the first time. As soon as we got outside, it was a special feeling, hot and humid, and I remembered my summers as a young man. People were everywhere, and there was no order, just a mess of people.

In Havana, almost everything was old, dilapidated, and underdeveloped, kind of like the USA in the early 1900s. The José Martí International Airport (HAV) was small. It had two terminals: 1 and 2; one for national and the other for international. Not many planes were coming or going. They were about one mile from each other, about twenty minutes from Havana centro, and they were rustic and very underdeveloped. The USA embargo on Cuba started in 1960, so since the '60s, Cubans weren't getting very much from the USA, and we in the USA were flourishing. We were moving forward so fast, and Cuba was standing still and moving backward. The airport had only two belts to pick up your luggage. Then you walked to the exit area, and they had two signs: nothing to declare (a green sign) or something to declare (a red sign).

As I left the airport, I saw two men, both very thin, wearing clothes that had been extinct in the USA since the '70s. They reminded me of the TV show *The Mod Squad*. I'm pretty sure they were secret police; remember, Cuba had a Russian influence for thirty years. They had developed many of the Soviet beliefs and procedures.

Havana had very few tall buildings and less new construction; some parts looked abandoned and war-torn. There was almost no industry; they were very far behind. The only things Cubans were allowed to do were drink, dance, and fuck. You were free to do it anytime, if you could find a way.

I noticed two guys who immediately caught my attention. They looked like New York City undercover drug cops from a '60s movie. One wore a two-tone wife-beater, beige with brown trim. I was pretty sure these guys were sent there to watch me. After getting our minivan and our "free" driver, we left the airport and started on our way to our hotel.

It wasn't more than three minutes before we saw two young girls riding their bikes on the other side of the road. Just like spics from a scene in *Scarface*, we were hanging out of the windows and throwing catcalls. Surprisingly, they smiled and waved...that was all we needed. We were all yelling for the driver to pull a U-turn and go back! He did, and we caught up to them quickly. I was the first one to get out of the sliding door, and I was pleasantly surprised. She was beautiful with her shoulder-length curly sandy-blond hair, bright blue eyes, white teeth, and a great tan. She was wearing cutoff blue jean shorts, and her legs were amazing. To be honest, I don't even remember what the other girl looked like, because I was blinded.

At the same time, Antonio was all over them like a vulture, as well as the other two guys. We arranged mostly through the driver to meet them at a spot later that evening, since we knew nothing. We agreed to meet at 7:00 p.m. They lived within a few miles of our hotel, which was on the complete other side of the city.

Once we were back in the van, we were all pumped up on adrenaline and male hormones. The adventure had begun about noon on a weekday. As we rolled through "Havana vieja" (old Havana), I really saw the poverty. The other areas outside of the airport were kind of rural with old, dilapidated factories and farming buildings, but this was poor. The building hadn't been maintained or even painted. Trash was everywhere in piles, and the people walking around looked like zombies. The driver knew where to go and took a curve along the beginning of the Malacon. We saw girls everywhere, black, white, brown, etc. They were dressed like whores, but they didn't even know it. Again, we all jumped out and pulled four girls into the van. It was on! Now we were ready to check into our rooms. The girls were on fire, flirting from the beginning and making us feel "special."

I had a thin white girl who was dressed like a 1980s pimp, and Antonio had a brown-skinned girl. It was on from the moment we got into the room. Antonio and I were sharing a bungalow, and the other two had theirs. I had my girl in the bedroom, and Antonio had his on the couch. She was really pouring it on; she made me feel like a champ, papi this and papi that. She asked me if I was of Cuban descent because I was muscular and had abs. She kept asking me all about myself and told me she wanted to be my girlfriend while I was there, and that she was crazy about me. She wasn't taking no for an answer, but I wasn't interested. I didn't want to make her feel bad, so I just avoided the issue.

A little while later, we left the room and went out to have a drink with Antonio and her friend. He had his bag of goodies and was carefully searching through it to give her a prize. He's one cheap MF, and I felt bad. He gave her maybe four dollars in junk.

At one point, he and I were alone in the hallway, and he said, "Hey, how do you feel about switching up?"

I said, "Oh, no way she'll go for that. She's in love with me."

He said, "No, it's okay. It was she who asked me if I wanted to switch up!"

Now I was the one who was hurt!

This was my first lesson about Cuba. I would learn all day, every day, but this was the first.

CUTOFF JEANS

By the time the four of us finally got rid of the other girls, it was getting dark. With all the excitement and commotion, we'd completely forgotten about the two girls we'd met on the bikes near the airport. We were starving too and hadn't eaten since the plane ride hours ago. We jumped in the van to go find them, but by now we were at least two hours late. It was pitch-black, and in Cuba, there aren't many streetlights. I figured there was no way they'd still be there. We didn't even have their phone numbers.

As we approached the meeting spot, the van's headlights cut through the darkness. We drove around a wide curve, and there, under a massive old willow tree with roots like something out of a fairy tale, stood the girls who were still waiting for us. Can you imagine that anywhere else in the world? It felt like stepping back into the 1950s.

They were dressed to the nines, looking wholesome, sexy, and clearly trying to make the best impression. I remember thinking how rough their lives must be if they were willing to wait this long. We turned the van around and headed back to our hotel.

That night, we all piled into our bungalow. We had drinks and food I'd brought with me. I offered them peanut butter, which they'd never tried. They were genuinely excited to share one of my favorites. Tono gave the girls little Snickers bars, acting like he was giving away gold.

He started getting drunk and a little macho, working hard to impress the prettier one, an eighteen-year-old named Diami Rodriguez. She was shy, soft-spoken, and still had an innocence about her. Antonio was laying it on thick, talking himself up like he was Donald Trump.

"I'm a doctor," he said. "I know people. In my country, it's about who you know. I'm going to have a very successful practice. Do you want to marry me?" He was drunk, cocky, and funny, but I felt sorry for her. Something about the way he talked to her bothered me. Eventually, I stepped in and pulled her away. Before long, he passed out cold.

Later, past midnight, I offered to have the driver take her home. On the way, we made out like a couple of teenagers. When we got to her place, we hugged and kissed outside for a while. She gave me her neighbor's phone number, which is common in Cuba, and we agreed to see each other the next day.

The truth? I was giddy. She was the only girl in all my time in Cuba with whom I ever felt any kind of emotional connection. Never again. I made sure after that to keep it strictly physical.

DIAMI

I spent a lot of time with her on that trip. I honestly don't know how, considering I was out at all hours and was rarely in the room unless I brought someone with me. She came along with us during the day, even hitting the tourist spots like El Morro, the old Spanish fort built to fight off the English.

One night, we went to the Comodoro nightclub, which was the hottest spot in Havana at the time. On the dance floor, she spotted another girl and said, "Qué lindos," pointing at her shoes. They were nothing special, just basic cloth sneakers from the Diplo store that cost maybe a few bucks. She asked if I could buy her a pair. She'd give me the money; she just wasn't allowed in the store. She also wanted tennis balls, if possible.

It broke my heart. It really did.

The next day, I took her there and spent a few hundred bucks, while a crowd waited outside wishing they could go in. I also gave her my jar of natural peanut butter, which she loved, especially with chocolate.

It was a bittersweet week. She was sweet, wholesome, and genuine...But I was buck wild and in no mood to settle down. The thought crossed my mind to invite her to Mexico, and it crossed it often, but it never went further.

I saw her only a few more times after that during later cigar trips. Once, I took her to El Aljibe for dinner. Somewhere between bites, she looked at me and asked if I was a gangster. I just smiled. I was dressed sharp, wore a Rolex (before it was stolen), and for a split second, I thought back to when I really was a gangster.

That was another life.

Although many women are in this story, they were always second. Business was always first and the most important thing in my life. I didn't go to Cuba looking to score with the "chicks."

But we were all young and single, so what the hell. Might as well have some fun.

SET IN MOTION

After a few days of being in Havana, we were visited by two Cuban men: one was related to a Cuban doctor living in Mexico. They came to pick up a bag we brought for them, and, as everyone in Cuba does to stay alive, they tried to sell us stuff.

This time it was Cuban cigars.

I bought two boxes: Cohiba Espléndidos and Montecristo #4. I mostly bought them just to help them out and not give away money.

Two boxes were fifty dollars (all currency is in dollars unless otherwise noted). These were common and popular. Cohiba was top of the line and had a retail value above $500 per box. But what did I know? At the time, I gave the money away. It was a gift—little did I know.

These guys were a sight to see: a short, shout white guy, Miguelito, five foot five with a thick head of hair styled like John Travolta in *Saturday Night Fever*, a pair of dark dress trousers from the 1960s, and a wife-beater tank top. The other guy, Ivan, was a tall Black guy also dressed like a cop from a 1960s film. They looked like cops I used to know when I was a kid. It was a sight for sore eyes, like the *Mod Squad* series from the '70s.

At that moment, it didn't really mean anything to me. Little did I know this was another one of those times when my fate was set in motion without me even knowing what was in store for me. Kindness and altruism would become the beginning of a brief career in the illegal cigar trade, which would be the beginning of my new life and the building block for who I would become.

That brief encounter and my sympathy for the two guys set my fate or destiny in motion. I didn't even pay attention to those two boxes for a while. I just put them inside a cabinet and closed the door.

There was something significant about that meeting—something that stuck with me. These Cuban guys could see how excited we all were about the "girls," and they felt compelled to educate us.

The tall Black man locked eyes with me and said, "Beware." He slowly passed his hand over his face from top to bottom. "Many women here have a beautiful face…" Then he moved his hand over his chest. "…but their hearts are ugly—cold and evil."

I understood immediately. Don't fall for anyone here, or you'll regret it.

BACK TO MY LIFE

When I got home, I continued building the business again. Before long, Cuba was no longer even a thought. As time passed, so did my trip to Cuba.

I was training and managing fighters, and let me tell you, that's a pain in the ass. Dealing with fighters and trainers is like herding cats with egos. Still, I was hustling. I'd started bringing Mexican boxing gear—gloves, pads, all that—back to the US on my trips. It wasn't much of a business, more like a hustle. It covered my travel, and maybe gave me a few bucks. I hated it.

I had bigger plans. I wanted to turn my small gym into something real—something big and cool. But I didn't have the cash, and I wasn't about to keep selling off what little I still had in the States. I didn't want all my eggs in one busted-up basket.

Next to my gym were a few vacant lots—not listed, not for sale. I wanted them all. I figured out a way to get the old, half-dead house next door. I convinced the owner to sell it to me for cash and even told him he could tear it down and keep everything—bricks, steel, wood, all of it. He agreed.

Watching him and his sons tear the place down brick by brick was something else. No machines—just hard labor. They salvaged maybe 80 percent of it. That cleared the space. The new property was about 1,500 square feet. There were still another 5,000 square feet next to it that I needed. I could already see it in my head—my expanded gym. I had the vision, the desire, and the will. What I didn't have was the money.

THE FIRST LETDOWN

At the time, my friend Brett was flush with cash and blowing it like a drunk on payday. I went to visit him. This was before the cigar hustle started. He was flying high, literally, on coke. He was in a great mood, so I laid out my plan for the gym.

He lit up, said he had $90,000 in cash and was looking for somewhere to invest it. He was all in. "You gotta name the basketball court after me!" he said. I agreed. Brett had been down to Mexico with me plenty of times. I thought it was a done deal.

That night, I went to bed floating. Finally, it was happening. I was already planning for the materials and layout in my head.

But the next morning, after the high wore off, so did his generosity. Drugs make people unstable. While high, he was all-in, but coming down, he was bitter and angry. He flipped the script. "You already have a life and a business. Now it's my turn!"

I was stunned. I pleaded with him, told him his money would be safer with me than in his closet. I even reminded him that if he ever got jammed up, I'd put my mother's house up for bond. It didn't matter. He was done.

A few months later, he threw that same money into a restaurant. Got a few free meals, played the big shot, and then lost it all. Later, he told me, "I should've given it to you."

Yeah. No shit.

LEO'S PROMISE

Out of the blue, I got a call from Leo, another dealer from Chicago, and a friend. He said he was looking for a house in Guadalajara, something special and underpriced.

He came down soon after. We were on my roof looking out over the city, and I pointed to the lots next door.

"You help me get my house, and I'll help you get those," he said.

Done. I even put down a deposit on the lots. Now I had skin in the game.

I called a woman I knew who sold property. She came through fast and found the perfect place: a private subdivision, mountain view, only $125,000. Thanks to a peso crash, his US dollars went a long way.

But this is Mexico, so of course, it got messy.

The seller tried to cut the broker out. She lost it, cussed him out, and threatened to walk. Leo was crushed. I told him to wait it out. I figured the guy was playing a game. And he was.

A month later, the broker's contract expired, and my house phone rang.

It was the seller. "Scott, can you get that guy back?"

I told him I wasn't sure.

"Please," he said. "I'll make it worth your while."

I called Leo. "If you make this happen," he said, "those lots are yours."

I was back on cloud nine.

I told him I'd need to drop a deposit to seal the deal. "Do it," he said. "It's as good as yours. I give you my word."

My wife overheard. "His word? He's Mexican. That's like an oxymoron."

She wasn't wrong. In Mexico, promises are like smoke.

REALITY HITS AGAIN

A few days later, the deal closed. Leo got his house. He came to my gym, and we went up to the roof. I showed him the lots again.

"What would I even do with this?" he asked.

"Not for you—for me," I told him. "You know I'll pay you back once I'm set."

He shook his head. "I can't. I spent too much on the house."

The seller had squeezed him for everything—furniture, cars, antenna, and even the damn dog. To top it off, Leo never gave my wife the finder's fee he'd promised.

I was pissed. I went after the seller. He tried to avoid me, but I don't get avoided. I got my $3,000, but I didn't get the help I thought I was getting.

I was turned down at the last minute by two friends, and I wasn't angry at either of them. I understand people and life. I knew I had to get it done myself. But I was still on the hook for that deposit, and if I couldn't come up with it fast, the seller would keep the money and sell it to someone else. My dream could vanish.

That was one of those "I should've known better" moments. A

reminder that no one's coming to save me. It's always been that way. We are all on our own. We each have our dreams and need to pursue them on our own.

Maybe that's why I'm strong. I've been let down more times than I can count, but I keep going. I get down, sure. Worn out. But then I reboot. My life's never been easy, and it sure as hell makes you cynical.

THE SPARK

On one of my return trips to Chicago, I stayed at my friend Brett's house. I remember landing at the airport on a freezing winter morning, dragging my huge, old, ugly suitcase stuffed with boxing gloves down the street. When I got to Brett's, he was still sleeping, so I just milled around until he finally came out. Like a scene out of an old movie, he came out in a Versace bathrobe, open at the front to show his bare, hairless chest and the weight of a thick braided gold chain. He loved designer everything—clothes, jewelry, furniture. A shameless snob, he demanded only the best, no matter the price.

The first thing he did was laugh at me, dragging that monster suitcase all over just to make a few bucks.

He asked what I made selling the boxing stuff. I told him it covered my travel and left me about $500 cash. He laughed again and said, "I make that per minute." He was a drug dealer and an addict. I wasn't. Not anymore, anyway. Still, it stung. He was right. It was peanuts. Almost a waste of time. I needed something else.

I spotted the morning newspaper on the table, picked it up, and froze. Wrapped inside was a kilo of cocaine, 2.2 pounds. My first instinct was to run, but I had nowhere else to stay.

I pulled my sleeves down over my hands, wiped the package feverishly to remove any prints, and tossed it back on the table. Then I just stared at it, thinking about the kind of money Brett was making. That opportunity was always there for me. All I had to do was give in.

A few weeks earlier, I'd given Brett a gift: a box of twenty-five Cohiba Espléndidos I'd bought in Cuba on my very first trip. Top of the line. Now that I was back, he asked me for more. I was surprised they were gone so fast, so I asked if he'd smoked them all.

"No," he said. "I sold them. Twenty-five bucks apiece."

That's when the lightbulb went on. I asked if he thought I could sell them too. He told me about a guy named Mark Farrow, who rode around on a scooter with a backpack full of cigars, filling orders all day at twenty-five dollars each—pockets stuffed with cash.

I sat there thinking, *Where would I start? Howard Frum Jewelers, that's where.* I'd known Howard for years. Everyone went to Howard's, and Howard knew everyone.

I had promised myself never to go back to street life. Not easy, considering I'd spent most of my life as a criminal. Two friends—both drug dealers—had already turned me down for a loan, even though they were drowning in money. Meanwhile, I was still well-connected in Mexico. If I wanted to, I could've jumped right back into my old game. It would've been easy. But I refused.

I'd made a promise to myself and, in a way, to my attorney, Thomas Garwood. He was one of those rare people sent into my life to save me. He didn't just defend me, he went above and beyond, pulling me out of the jaws of the Georgia legal system. He believed in me. He trusted me. I felt an overwhelming debt of gratitude. I would not let him down. Even if I never saw him again, even if he never knew what I did or didn't do, the forces that sent him to me would know. That was enough.

So I stayed clean. I took the high road.

But cigars? That was something my conscience could live with. I remember thinking, *Who really gives a shit about someone selling cigars? This could be my path forward.* I didn't know a damn thing about them, but fuck it, I'd learn. And I dove in headfirst.

I didn't realize it at the time, but buying those first two boxes of cigars out of pity was a turning point. Then, finding out Brett had sold them for $25 each—$625 for one box—sealed it. From that moment, I was all in.

I had decided it was time to build a real life. I had ambitions and the drive to keep pushing. Cigars gave me a middle ground—a way to use my contacts, my work ethic, and my energy to create the kind of life I wanted.

THE BUY

I was a man on a mission with no time to waste. As soon as I got back to Mexico, I asked around and eventually made my first contact: Arturo Brigante, a Cuban living in Mexico and selling cigars to businessmen. He showed up with his helper, carried himself like a boss, made a few quick gestures, and the kid went out to the car, returning with two suitcases full of Habanos.

Don't be fooled—it wasn't easy to find him. It was a process. I reached out to a lot of people before someone finally knew of him. At first, he was just a myth, a rumor, but soon enough, I tracked him down. He was perfect for the role—the Cuban cigar salesman—like he'd been cast for it. And me? An ex-felon with the right amount of grit to play my part. The whole thing was starting to take shape.

All I had to my name was $4,400 in cash. I bought forty boxes from Arturo at $110 each. I was willing to risk it all. That was the beginning of everything.

I had only been back in Mexico a few days, but it already felt like an eternity. On Thursday, I made my first buy. By Saturday morning, I was in a car headed toward the US border at Laredo. Riding with me were two friends: my good friend Antonio (we took his car) and Oscar, a real character.

I knew nothing about cigars. Nothing. My only references were a recent copy of *Cigar Aficionado* and an old memory of my Italian gangster-like Uncle Joe, who had a cigar in his mouth until the day he died. None of that mattered. I was all in. Headfirst into the deep end.

Chapter Three

FIRST RUN—ALL OR NOTHING

THIS WAS MY FIRST OFFICIAL CIGAR RUN. I MIGHT HAVE BEEN new to cigars, but I wasn't new to playing cops and robbers. I knew the underworld.

We got stopped by the cops and federals too many times to count. They once made us wait at a checkpoint for a few hours. It was a battle to get the cigars to the border. Mexico is a corrupt place where all the cops have their hands out.

This trip was the first of many. None of them were exactly alike, but they were all the same: shitty, low-rent hotels, people I didn't want to trust, constant bribes, the fear of being caught, and always finding new ways across the border.

We finally made it to Laredo, Mexico (the border with Laredo, Texas) and settled into a five-dollar-a-night room. The next morning, we spread out to look for options for crossing the cigars to the other side of the border.

Oscar returned with a guy he met somewhere on the street. The border towns are gritty, to say the least. He brought him back to our room. The guy gave me an uneasy feeling, and I was mad that Oscar was so stupid to bring him to where we were staying. The guy said he had a small raft he used to transport illegals across the river. He would use his raft, and we needed to be on the other side to receive the cargo. If he didn't look like such a scumbag, I might have done it, but in the end, we got rid of him and quickly left the hotel with our bags. I knew he might come back to rob us or bring the law to extort us.

That guy proposed that he had some truck inner tubes and a rope system. He would load up the bags on the tubes and send them across the river to me, waiting on the other side. I know it's almost comical to think about, but I had bad thoughts. The worst is that Oscar was trying to convince me! Wet, cold, and rainy, a few miles outside of civilization, doing something really stupid and messy. When I think about it, it's almost unbelievable.

We then met a guy who lived directly in front of the river who claimed he could bring the cigars across easily, and I went for it. The problem was these guys weren't what you would call brilliant, but they managed to get them to the other side, and it was a mess!

It was winter in Texas. It gets cold and overcast, and it was forty degrees and raining during the daytime. They crossed the river with the two suitcases over their heads in plain sight. They left them in the brush behind a park that was at the border, literally on the river's edge. Then they simply went back across and into their house. Just a short time earlier, I had walked across the border bridge, and I saw a few border agents looking and watching the river areas with binoculars. This was a shit show. I didn't want to get caught, and this was bad.

It was a strategic nightmare. The border bridge was half a block away, and the agents often used binoculars to scan the area. There was a huge parking lot for the mall, and a tall hotel I thought could easily be used by the cops to watch. We waited and waited. We walked around, we staked it out, and waited some more. I was almost sure it was a trap, but eventually we decided to go for it. We pulled the car up and loaded the bags in twenty seconds and disappeared into traffic.

Once we got to a hotel, I opened the bags and took inventory. I was missing four boxes, and the others were kind of beat up from the trip. I would later learn how to package them correctly to keep them fresh in a protected box. I was so angry, I was about to explode. It's so hard to do anything in Mexico, and with Mexicans, the chances of something going wrong or getting burned are almost 100 percent.

I had paid the guys $400 to get the bags across the river, and losing boxes wasn't part of my plan. It took me at least an hour and a half to get there, cross the border again, and get back to the shithole where they lived. I was ready for battle. I wanted to break every bone in the guy's body. I went back to their house, but by the time I got there, they were already high as could be. The look on his stupid face just made me realize who I was dealing with. It was a waste of time to even go back, but I learned a few lessons.

It took me another two hours to get back across the border and to my room at some other shithole motel.

I was now prepared to travel all the way to Chicago. There was still at least one more border checkpoint before I could say I was in the USA. This was yet another hurdle.

To my surprise, Oscar said he wanted to take the trip to Chicago with me, but he was broke, and we knew he needed a job. So I bought him a Greyhound ticket to Chicago. He only had the clothes on his back and my cigars. Antonio and I closely followed the bus. We went through the next checkpoint, but Oscar's bus was stopped, and all the passengers had to claim their bags and stand next to them. I was worried I would lose my cargo. They ran the drug-sniffing dogs along the bags and the passengers, and I was very concerned the dog would bring its attention to the cigars, and they would get confiscated.

They ran the dog back and forth a few times, and that was it. No problem, no issue. I watched Oscar get back on the bus, and I also saw the bags get reloaded. It was a great feeling; the hardest parts were over. The two-hour drive to San Antonio was easy, and I almost felt intoxicated. We followed Oscar to the Greyhound station. Then we met and made plans before he departed for Chicago.

Oscar was a white Mexican. He could have passed for almost any ethnicity, and he sometimes told people he was Italian or Irish.

He spoke perfect English and Spanish, he was funny and very likable, but he lied and omitted truths. He had worn the same clothes since leaving Guadalajara two or three days earlier: black dress pants, shiny black dress shoes, white sport socks, and a white sweatshirt. The sweatshirt had a few stains, which made him look messy and like an immigrant. He was so happy. He would throw his hands up into the air and yell, "Chiiii Caaaaaggggo, here I come." Antonio and I would laugh our asses off. He was half clown, and I was just figuring it out now. Tono had already told me he was "off," and he would laugh and point out details, but I didn't really care. It was better for Oscar to take the torturous two-day bus ride than for me. I knew he needed some money, and I felt okay with him.

I told him, "NEVER let the bags out of your sight. You must keep them under your control, be careful when you stop and switch buses, and you must keep your eyes on them."

I gave him the phone number of my cousin Marty. I told him to call Marty once he was in Chicago, and Marty would come and pick up the suitcases. It was complicated for me, and I didn't have time to plan well. I was new to this game, and I had to learn the specific details related to this new part of my life. I knew the streets, and I was already a pretty good businessperson, but this was new.

Oscar got on the bus, and it drove away. Antonio and I headed back to the Mexican border on our way to Guadalajara. I was actually calm and felt like everything was going well. I got back to GDL and waited for news that didn't come. I knew Oscar's arrival date and time. I was waiting, and he didn't call me. I called my cousin, and he hadn't heard from him either. Now I was impatient. It had already been twenty-four hours since he should have arrived.

I finally got his call. The bags were lost!

He said, "The Black guy in Tennessee, where I switched buses, told me he would take care of them."

I snapped. Boy-o-boy, was Antonio right. This guy was special.

I got a ticket as fast as I could, and I flew to Chicago. Oscar was staying at a five-dollar-a-night flophouse on Roosevelt and Wabash in downtown Chicago; it was worse than a shithole. I got to Chicago early in the morning and took the subway to where he was staying. To my relief, the suitcases had arrived, and Oscar had them. Oscar was still wearing the same clothes.

THE ROLEX KING

We immediately went a few blocks north to 5 South Wabash. It's an important building in the jewelry world of Chicago, and Howard Frum has his showroom there. It's an amazing place with lots of people coming and going, phones ringing, and people talking.

Howard's a real character who specializes in used Rolex watches, but he's involved in the jewelry business. Howard can entertain anyone twenty-four hours a day. He knows everyone, or they know him. I have a saying, "If you don't know Howard, you're not from Chicago." I love Howard. He has always been good to me. He's smooth and easy to deal with. A gentleman.

We walked into Howard's about noon, and as always, it was alive. I eventually got Howard's attention, and he took me into his back office. I brought the suitcases and told him what I had. He immediately started making calls. He was all in before I even explained everything. I sold all forty boxes that day!

I immediately got a flight back to GDL with my $12,600 in cash. I was pumped up. I was now ready to get serious.

I got home and immediately contacted my Cuban connection. He brought 120 boxes to my office, and I bought them all, this time at $100 per box, which meant he was out of inventory. He had never made sales like he was making with me. We were both happy at that moment. Everything was just beginning.

I am a quick learner, and I was already learning so much information: brands, sub-brands, sizes, shapes, dates, stamps, factories, seals. It's a fucking science. Cigars are by no means simple. They are very complex and unique, and to sell them at the highest price, you need to know what you're doing.

BORDER RATS

The next few months, I was in constant motion: one run after another, always some new thing going wrong or trying to find a better way to get the cigars into the US.

Oscar had been boasting that he had been a player in the drug world a few years ago. He claimed he had an inside advantage at the Nogales border. We went to Nogales, Mexico, which borders Nogales, Arizona.

The trip went as planned. My suitcase was stored in the driver's private sleeping cabin. I didn't even have to deal with the "federals." Once we arrived at the border town, we got a cheap hotel room. Oscar took off for the entire day, and I was left at a sleazy, transient shithole.

I was the only foreigner at the motel. It was a 1970s U-shaped hotel right in the center of Nogales, Mexico. While I waited for Oscar to return, I was approached by several different guys.

"Hey, *wheto* (white guy). You're with Oscar, right?"

Oscar had been showing off, pretending to be doing big business with a gringo. As it turns out, Oscar did have a past in Nogales. He knew a few people and had been smuggling his drugs from there to Los Angeles a few years earlier. These guys wanted to sell me their products. Even though they believed me to be Oscar's customer, they were trying to steal my business.

The border towns of Mexico are a unique place, all seedy, and the last stop for everyone and everything trying to get into the USA. There are always a lot of people just sitting idle and waiting for word that their passage is scheduled. There are a lot of questionable characters, and it's dangerous. You have criminal bandits and the official ones. Police and federal agents all want what you have, and life is less than cheap.

These places get people from all over Mexico and the world who want to cross into the USA, 95 percent illegal. It's where a majority of drugs from around the world get ready to cross into the USA. Millions, if not billions of dollars, are stashed throughout these cities. There are cops of every kind just waiting around, using snitches and lookouts to tell them what's going on. It's not that these cops actually care what anyone is doing. They just want their share of the money.

I've been to almost every Mexico–USA border town, and they're all the same with minor distinctions, but the same shithole. I'm not saying there aren't good people in all these places; there are, but they are a minority. It's made up of bandits, crooked cops, a crooked government, drug dealers, and prostitutes. Many people have ended up there and are stuck; no more money and no options. I had plenty of time to sit around thinking about all this while Oscar was gone.

He finally returned late at night and told me he was looking for the guys who did his smuggling. He brought another random guy to our room, and he went on about how the passage was difficult at the moment and showed us an area close to the hotel that looked like a scene from a Terminator movie, complete with gates, fences, barbed wire, and cameras. He said maybe he could cross there.

Not a fucking chance, I thought.

Oscar then told me about the guys he was looking for. "Pollo" was the head of the group of young guys who spent most of their nights crossing drugs and sometimes people. He lived on top of a hill that looked directly over the border wall.

The next morning, Oscar and I took a city bus across town and up the hill to look for him. We found him at his house in the "Buenos Aires" neighborhood, basically all dirt roads with mostly unfinished homes.

Pollo told us there was a lot of movement on the USA side, and he hadn't tried to cross for a few days. We hung out and bullshitted for a while, and then he went to the edge of the hill and just stared out and almost meditated. He then decided we would take the journey together. So about four or five of us started walking. I really wasn't sure what we were doing, and I just went along.

The border "wall" was only present for a short distance near the border crossing, then it just stopped. We only had to make our way around some makeshift barriers and a few low barbed-wire fences, similar to what you see on a farm. We walked through the desert, up and down the hills. I was warned before we started to watch for rattlesnakes and scorpions. I tied up the bottom of my jeans, tucked my shirt in, and walked.

It probably took two hours, and then we were officially in Nogales, Arizona.

We walked up to a very nice subdivision with nice houses, in a nice neighborhood. It was a little surreal. We came from literal dirt roads and extreme poverty to an affluent neighborhood in a quick walk. When we arrived on a dead-end street, Pollo told me, "This is where you'll pick us up. Be here at 3:00 a.m., and we'll load you up."

We then walked back to Mexico without a problem. I packed the backpacks as well as I could, trying to keep the load tight, with no room for the cigars to move, to avoid noise and wear and tear on the boxes. I sometimes used cardboard, towels, or even clothes.

We then brought them back to Pollo's house. This time, he was on the edge of the hill in deep thought, kind of like an ancient ritual before battle. He said he wasn't so sure anymore, and he didn't feel it.

I was coming apart at the seams. I'm not a patient person, and I was already worn out from the trip and the bullshit. I didn't have many options. It's not like there's an office you can go to and hire a few "coyotes" for the night. We went back to the room and waited.

The next day, we had a new option. They told me about the drain tunnels that run from the Mexican side all the way to the US side. It was a dry season, so there was no need to worry about drowning to death. They said it took longer to walk because they had to make sure to walk on the sides of the tunnel, kind of on an angle, because there were sensors on the bottom. To avoid detection, they had to stay out of the middle. The tubes are round and made of ribbed metal, so it's difficult to stay on the side.

I decided to have a woman fly to Tucson to meet me, because it would make me less likely to get searched. I got a ride from someone to Tucson, and I wanted to see the next checkpoint, and this gave me a chance to drive through it and see what was up.

The checkpoint was just a small, primitive space, a kind of mobile home office with a laminate roof, a few border agents, and a dog. They waved me right through, but I saw them ask someone to open their trunk. My odds were good that I would just get waved through, but I thought it would look better if I had a woman with me. I picked her up at the Tucson airport and returned to Nogales.

I got us a room at a hotel on the US side in Nogales, Arizona. It was on. The guys were bringing the bags across tonight, and I needed to be at a certain street at 5:00 a.m.

It was so funny. I was waiting in my car where they told me to be, and out of nowhere, I saw a head pop out of the sewer drain at the curb, just like a gopher popping its head out. I pulled my car up, got out, and they handed me my bags. I loaded them into my car, and that was it. My cigars were now in the USA.

I went back to the hotel and hustled all the bags into my room. I had asked for a room closest to the rear/side door of the hallway for just this reason. I didn't want to make noise or call any attention to myself. I got the bags into the room and tried to sleep, but I couldn't rest.

We got ourselves ready, and I had to carefully pack all the bags into the truck. It's better not to weigh the car down and definitely not have any bags or anything in plain sight. I also had to consider the well-being of my product. I didn't want to leave my expensive cigars in the hot sun.

We started our one-hour drive from Nogales to Tucson. I used a nice hanger from the hotel and hung a suit coat on the hanger in the back of the car. I wore a white shirt, a tie, and dress pants. The woman was also well-dressed. We were waved through without incident and on our way to Tucson.

TUCSON TO CHICAGO

We got to a motel in Tucson, and I quickly unloaded the bags into the room. At that point, I still hadn't learned much about cigars. I had a notion they were an organic product and needed certain care. Once inside the room, I emptied all the backpacks. When all the cigar boxes were unloaded and on a table in the room, it hit me. *Wow, this is a lot of cigars.* The pile was huge and impressive. For a moment, I felt the gravity of the whole thing. I thought, *What the fuck am I getting into?*

I was still on federal paper, and if I got caught in any type of trouble, I could go back to jail. I always had in the back of my mind that this was only cigars, not a big deal. Not like selling or smuggling drugs. So I was thinking and this was a way to convince myself that it was ok. This is what was always in the back of my mind, even if I got caught, was it really a big deal?

I took all the boxes into the bathroom and turned on the hot water to start a humidified atmosphere in hopes of giving them correct care. I also didn't want this huge pile of cigar boxes in plain sight. They were around the size of a kilo of coke (known on the streets as a "brick") and the same size packages as weed.

I went through a lot of suitcases and backpacks while dealing with the cigars. Many just disappeared, and others were abandoned. I tried to preserve them if possible, but I sometimes had to just walk away. Although it was common for me to pack one into the other in multiple layers, I would stuff the empty backpacks in wherever they would fit.

I bought tickets from Tucson to Chicago. I had no idea what to expect, but this was the 1990s; security was still lax, and technology was nothing like it is today. I was just not sure what would happen, so I checked the bags and flew to Chicago. I retrieved my checked bags without a problem.

Once in Chicago, I went to my mother's apartment in the western suburbs, about thirty minutes from downtown Chicago. Oscar arrived, and we all took a ride. I loaded up my mother's old beater of a car and headed to see Howard. I got to Howard's shop, and as always, it was rocking. He even had an old Black man shining shoes. This guy was just another character who fit in well at Howard Frum Jewelers. Howard's is a busy place. Like all jewelry shops, he has a buzzer to get in and out; that thing is buzzing all day. It's sometimes difficult to get Howard's attention. He's like the Energizer bunny: phone calls every five minutes, employees asking questions, customers coming and going all the time.

I brought the very attractive Spanish-speaking woman with me, as a prop, if you will. She gave me a bit of credibility, first because I speak Spanish, and second because she was Cuban. Well, to be honest, she wasn't even Cuban, but she looked like Daisy Fuentes (a Cuban American actress/model), and she only spoke Spanish, so I got out of it what I wanted.

I just kind of opened my suitcases and set some boxes out, and before long, I was selling. Howard got on the phone, made calls, and I became very popular. It reminded me of my drug-dealing days... sometimes you get treated like a celebrity.

But then I started to have some technical issues.

A LOT OF BULLSHIT

Americans are an interesting study. We had the most amazing country in the history of the world. Most of us have to go to school and educate ourselves, but some Americans I sold to took bullshit to the next level!

I started getting the guys who thought they knew it all. They scrutinized me and my product, and then the bullshit started. The only information any of them had was bullshit they read in magazines. None of them knew what they were talking about, but they believed they did. They questioned the boxes, the color of the cigars (tones), and they questioned the stamps on the bottom of the boxes, everything. They made my life uncomfortable. I didn't have answers. I just didn't know enough to defend myself, but like everything in my life, I was going to learn and become great at it.

I felt attacked. I wanted to start beating people, but I couldn't. They more than deserved it. I lost many sales because of people putting in their two cents, and the potential customer getting scared off.

While I was at Howard's, a few celebrities came in: Ron Rivera, of the Chicago Bears football team, and actor/celebrity Joe Pantoliano (a.k.a. Joey Pants). There were cops, politicians, business owners, judges, lawyers, newscasters, TV personalities, thugs, and gangsters all the time.

Wow, I thought. *It's a flashback to the 1980s. This is the cocaine of the '90s. These guys are crazy. They will pay $350 to $1,200 per box for something they're going to burn. It's the same as burning money!* "Gotta have it" was their attitude. I couldn't believe it, but I just rode the wave. Well, I created part of the wave myself.

I was now out and about more than at Howard's office; I didn't want to be predictable. Never let people know your schedule or habits. It wasn't a good idea to have all my inventory in one place at the same time. One hundred twenty boxes of cigars looks like a lot. In money, it was worth about $40,000.

After about a week of running around and working my ass off, I had approximately forty boxes left. I had visited all the customers I had, and I really didn't have all the right brands and sizes the customers wanted. Again, cigar customers are a bit opinionated and closed-minded. Many of the "new" cigar smokers are just fad seekers following the flow. Most of the customers had money, lots of money, but some were just normal guys making a living.

I met one of my customers on this second trip, photographer Mark Hauser. I went to his studio (he also lived there). He was pretty informative about cigars. He loved the #2 cigar or the torpedo, Montecristo #2, or Diplomaticos. He told me he wanted to buy any Torpedoes that I got, and I sold him the few boxes I had and agreed to see him next time.

One of the people Howard called to tell him the cigars had arrived was a Jewish guy named Steve. He rushed over and tried to bum-rush me. He was aggressive and a pain in the ass. He wanted them all. He wanted me to sell exclusively to him. He would pay me $300 per box. He would buy every box I could get, and on and on. Since I was just getting started, and all I really wanted was to make some money, I said, "Sure."

I sold him the remaining boxes (they weren't the best or most sought after), and he gave me a check for $12,000, which meant this trip was almost over. I got cash from some customers, and some paid by check. Since I was only getting started, I had to fine-tune all the operational details, so I deposited the check into my mother's account.

I had about $20,000 on me besides the several checks I deposited and the large check that Steve gave me. I flew back to Mexico, where I had my business and my family. I had my gym, I still worked with a few boxers, and I was giving kickboxing classes a few times a week. Whenever I got back, I was always behind on my work and had to work double-time to get caught up. Sometimes I just got lost in the hustle.

Back then, it took about a week for a check to clear, and maybe two weeks for an out-of-state check to clear. I got the news from my mother that the bank had called her to let her know the $12,000 check had bounced, and there was no money to cover it.

I could feel my blood boil.

I immediately called Howard Frum. Steve fucked him too. I'm sure Howard called him. I eventually got Steve on the phone, and he played tough and was really pissing me off. He told me he canceled the check because he found out I had sold a few boxes to Mark Hauser. He reminded me that we had agreed I would sell only to him. He was having a baby fit!

I explained that I had initially arrived with 120 boxes and that it was obvious I had sold many before meeting him. It was still a bullshit move for him to cancel the check. I called my childhood friend and longtime criminal accomplice, Stuart Glaser. Stu and I have known each other since we were kids; he is a Jew and knows "everyone." I explained to Stu what happened (I was probably screaming and animated). He made a few calls and found out who the guy was and what he was about. Stu showed up at Steve's office with two other guys from the neighborhood. Remember, we were gangbangers, thugs, and gangsters while growing up.

I'm pretty sure Steve got the message. The check cleared two days later.

I never sold another cigar to that prick. He tried to buy all the time, but I wouldn't deal with him.

FRONT PAGE NEWS

Smuggling cigars sounds glamorous, but a lot of it is waiting, worrying about your merchandise, and sitting in terrible motels in the middle of nowhere.

On another trip, I boarded the bus with 375 boxes of Cuban cigars, divided into twelve suitcases with backpacks stuffed into the suitcases. It was much smarter to use suitcases to travel to the border and not use the green military-style backpacks that would make people take a second look. So I saved the backpacks for when I got to the border, and then at the house, I'd pack them up with the cigars. Carrying fifteen to twenty military-green backpacks loaded, all squared off, just doesn't look normal.

The bus ride was about a forty-hour trip, long and slow. I found myself literally in the middle of nowhere. It's a dry, dusty, hot climate in this area of the world, and the climate is very similar to Phoenix, Arizona. Now I'm here, alone, in a place that almost no one in the world has ever even heard of, with twelve suitcases.

This was now the product of my labor, and I had gone directly to Cuba for these cigars. I had put all my gains and winnings back into the product. I had traveled to Cuba twice for loads of cigars, and I hadn't slept very much over the last few weeks. I could feel that my batteries were low, and I was pushing it.

After a two-hour wait, I boarded a bus to Nogales, Mexico. Everything was fine until I arrived at the Nogales bus station. There were cops, and they saw one guy alone with a mountain of suitcases. I was hauling what looked like a lot of "stuff," and I was a white foreigner, so they would automatically assume drugs (weed).

I was held in place at the side of the bus, in the lane between two buses, no witnesses at all, except the drivers, but they don't have a voice or vote, really. I was calm and told them I was a cigar salesman, and all I had were cigars. Regardless of what I said, they couldn't believe me. They have seen and heard it all. Who would really say, "I've got my bags loaded with weed?"

They held me for a few hours, a few other cops came and went, and they were all disappointed to learn the cases contained only cigars. They searched random cases. This was just commercial business, nothing more. Cuban cigars were not at all prohibited in Mexico (on the contrary, there were official Habanos distributors). I ended up giving them 400 pesos, which was about fifty dollars at the time, but I was tired of the inconvenience and the bullshit. All they really wanted was a piece of everything. Even if the suitcases were full of drugs, I could probably have negotiated my way out of it.

I got back to the same shithole motel we stayed at the other time, and Oscar was already in town. It was hot as hell and dry.

That evening, I got about eighteen backpacks ready to go. The guy on the hill didn't feel comfortable with me coming to his house. He said it was already noticed, and he was asked questions. He told me he would come to get the bags from now on. He said things had been pretty smooth, and they would do the crossing tonight. Oscar offered to accompany them on this crossing. He was a Mexican national and had a green card, which meant he could come and go as he pleased.

The protocol at this time was that the illegals would be rounded up throughout the night and then all brought back to the border crossing in the early morning and released like fish. They were directed across the border, free and ready to prepare for their next crossing attempt. Many people spend extended periods of time in the border towns waiting to get across, getting caught and released over and over again.

It had been three days since I left my home, wife, and two small daughters. I was already way behind on sleep and rest, and with the lack of good meals and all the little bullshit, I felt exhausted. Dealing with Oscar could probably cause anyone to go out of their mind too.

The guy from the hill came to pick up the bags. He was surprised to see so many bags, and he just looked at me and again asked, "*Weto*, (white guy) why don't you just take weed and drugs like everyone else?"

I just smiled and said, "Not interested. I've been there and done that, and I made a promise and will keep my promise."

They didn't know what to charge me. They normally charge forty dollars per pound of weed for the crossing; we settled on $600. He told me to be at the place where the road ends at 5:00 a.m., the place that we walked to before, in the nice neighborhood with all the big homes. I crossed to the USA side of the border and again got a rental car. I was ready for the load to come to me.

As anyone can imagine, I couldn't sleep. I was burning energy at a fast pace, and I just couldn't rest.

I got to the pickup location and found a quiet spot to park the car and wait; it was dark and quiet. I wasn't there very long, and I certainly didn't cause any attention or make any noise, but the dogs in the area started going crazy. It sounded like an orchestra.

I decided to drive a bit, and when I pulled out, I could now see action.

The dogs were going crazy, the lights were on in homes, and the neighborhood was waking up. I saw police and official cars racing around the neighborhood.

I had to decide, fast, what to do. First, I had to get the fuck out of there. I drove away and then went back. I needed to know what was going on. Fuck, my cigars. I had no way to know what had happened. I couldn't just make a call. I didn't have any way to get close enough either. I had no reason to be there. Although I was an American citizen, I wasn't from these parts and I definitely didn't belong in this subdivision. I was also on parole and didn't want to be questioned.

I went to the place where the buses came and waited. I was hoping to see Oscar, but I didn't. I was now concerned for him and my cigars. What had happened? I went back and forth between my hotel, the border, and the pickup area. I probably did this twenty times. I finally gave in and crossed the border back into Mexico. I had to figure out what happened. I didn't have any options but to go back.

Once I got back to the room on the Mexican side, I found Oscar. He was outside the hotel talking to someone. I was animated and strung out on adrenaline. I asked him what happened, and he told me, "There were twenty guys in their group, they walked single file and didn't talk or make noise, but they must have either stepped on a sensor or been seen by night vision. When they got close to the pickup spot, they were ambushed by border patrol. He said it was a real show. The agents chased the guys around in circles, and the guys would drop their bags and run, then come back around and grab their same bags as the cops were still running around.

He said they had lost about 50 percent of the bags. I was crushed. I was already so beat, and this just drained me a little more.

None of the guys were caught, and they returned to Mexico with what they could. They would attempt to cross the bags again when they felt the time was right.

I had to sleep. It was about 10:00 a.m. now, and I desperately needed sleep.

I woke up a few hours later, went out, called my wife, and told her what had happened. I was now almost empty. She could hear it in my voice. I was not my usual self. She said, "Just come home," and I did think about it. I thought about just throwing in the towel.

Easy money? Fuck no, this was hard labor. I don't know anyone who would be able to deal with all this bullshit.

But I just couldn't stop. I needed this, and I couldn't build my business without a push.

ADDING SALT TO THE WOUND

When I stepped outside looking for something to eat, that's when I saw a man sitting on a bench, reading the newspaper. Even from a distance, I could see the front page, and it hit me like a punch to the gut. A giant photo of my cigars. Clear as day. Bold black letters screamed across the top:

"INCAUTAN 4,874 PUROS CUBANOS."

"Seized 4,874 Cuban Cigars." Just like that.

It felt like the paper was mocking me. A finger in my eye. I walked up to him and asked to see it. He must've read my face, because before I could say more, I smacked the paper with the back of my hand and said, "That's my load. The gringos grabbed it last night."

He looked at me and nodded. "I'm sorry. I know the feeling," he said, and then handed me the paper. "Keep it. For the memories."

I was so pissed, I jumped in my car and headed straight for the border. I didn't care about anything except getting something familiar to eat on US soil. Once I crossed, I went directly to a place I knew.

And then came the insult to injury.

I sat down at the restaurant and immediately spotted another newspaper sitting on a nearby table—like it was waiting for me. Calling me out. I walked over, picked it up, and there it was again.

Front page. A picture of one of my specialty cigars. The long one—twelve inches. I had bought it for a specific customer. And now, there it was in the paper, laid out with a ruler next to it, showing off its size like a trophy.

Like the universe flipping me off.

It was like they were saying, "Go home. Quit. Get a regular life. You're done."

But not me. I can take more than most.

After that, we had to sit and wait for another three days; they just had us waiting. This was so common in these places, people were just waiting. I finally had my cigars on the other side; they got there without anything happening. I loaded them into the truck without the bags. I was beat. I was also down and out, thinking about the whole process to get here, and now I've lost half of all the work I've done.

The expenses along the way really add up. I'm paying for everything for everyone. All travel accommodations, airfare, hotels, food, cars, buses, gas, and even entertainment. These trips in total are expensive and taxing on me. Now with this 50 percent loss of my cigars, I'm not feeling high at this point.

Then, once we finally made it to Chicago and I started calling customers, bang, the first guy I called, Bill, a new car salesman and the nephew of the owner, as soon as he heard my voice, he started at me.

"These cigars are shit. I can't smoke them. They are too tight. I just can't get anything, no matter how hard I try."

I had to think on my feet, and I said, "Slow down, that's why I'm calling you, I wanted to check to see if they were okay. I had heard about that batch being less than perfect. What others would you like? I'll come and exchange them tomorrow."

Then I got off the phone and exploded like a steam engine. I had to get this shit together. I couldn't keep going through this. It was too much bullshit, all the time.

I was pissed off, but I took it. I knew I had to keep my customers happy, and I had to take this loss and several more like it. But it showed them I was solid, and in the end, it was worth it.

Chapter Four

UNDERSTANDING CIGARS

AS SOON AS I REALIZED THE MONEY I COULD MAKE SELLING cigars, I returned to Cuba with Eduardo and began to research the "world-famous Cuban cigars." Eduardo had told me he knew where the Romeo & Julieta factory was, so we went there first. I figured out quickly that there are many people selling cigars on the "streets," hence the term "Street Cigars." These people were everywhere. They waited around any potential tourist attractions and offered boxes of cigars at a huge discount. Obviously, they'll stick it to someone if they have the opportunity.

Some cigar factories have a store open to the public, and some do not. The most well-known and accessible to tourists is the Partagás factory and Casa de Habanos. All of them are owned by the state, the government. The cigars in the factory are much more expensive than anything on the street, by far. At that time, a box of Cohiba Espléndidos cost $550 in the store and $25 on the street. The problem is that the street cigars are made by people who don't care about quality. They want your money and nothing else. They also don't have the resources to do everything correctly. Of course, some people will know quality and pay attention to detail, but you must know what you're looking for too.

The other issue was that the cigar places didn't have an unlimited amount of cigars available to the public. Most of their business was direct to their distributors around the world; they got their orders filled first.

I was thrown off for a moment or two. *I can't just walk in and buy what I want?* I pretty much spent twenty-four hours a day on my mission. I wasn't there to have fun. As always, I started learning more and more, met people, and made contacts. I had a huge advantage; I spoke Spanish, and I was a street guy. I've made my life through contacts and friends; plus, I have 100 percent willpower, discipline, and drive. I'm relentless when I have focus and I'm interested.

I met a university professor, Capi; he was in his midthirties, chubby with a full beard and mustache. He had family in Santa Clara, where he said they have access to cigars, good ones made with quality and correctly. Santa Clara is a small town of about 250,000, and it's about a three-hour drive to Havana. He assured me he would get cigars and also offered me *facturas* (invoices) for my cargo.

You see, the Cuban government was just now starting to protect its cigar industry, and it was becoming a very important part of their economy. As the cigar craze got more popular, Cuba took advantage and rode the wave. As a tourist, you were allowed only $1,000 per person in cigar purchases to pass through customs on your way out. I ended up buying seventy boxes of cigars from Capi, and I paid somewhere around twenty dollars per box. He gave me the fake receipts, and we filled them out by hand. They were just numbered green receipts from a booklet, and the receipts had the name of some cigar shop.

My week had gone well. I made a few contacts, bought seventy boxes of cigars, and learned more about cigars and the business. I didn't know it yet, but my education was just beginning. There is a lot to know about cigars. I was still poorly informed, but we managed to have some fun too.

There was still a lot I could learn from my first cigar supplier, Arturo Brigante. He had started coming around more often, and we were becoming real friends (we still are to this day). By then, I was gaining a reputation as the guy who could move cigars, and I was getting tight with the Cuban community in town. I'd met around forty Cubans—men and women—and let me tell you, the women weren't average. These were the kind of women men started wars over. A lot of them were escaping Cuba for Mexico, and plenty were drop-dead gorgeous.

Arturo would call me whenever someone came back from Cuba with cigars, trying to line up a deal. Sometimes I'd hang out with his father, Arturo Sr.—a character straight out of Havana central casting. He was about seventy, with graying hair slicked back like he'd stepped out of the 1950s, a thick gold chain resting on his chest, a white "dago T" tank top, and always—always—a cigar hanging from his lips. He held court from his chair, a kind of Cuban throne, with a beat-up Styrofoam cooler sitting beside it. Inside, he'd rigged a few wires across the middle to make a grate, a little water in the bottom, and cigars laid neatly on top—his own homemade humidor.

He told me he'd been smoking since he was a kid, and according to him, all the brand-name fuss was nonsense. "They're all Cuban," he said, "all the same tobacco." When I told him how obsessed American buyers were with brands, boxes, and labels, he just laughed, a deep, smoker's laugh.

"That's for rich men who need something to brag about," he said.

And you know what? He was right. If it was rolled in Cuba, it was a Cuban cigar—end of story. Sure, batches could vary, but most of the difference was in the smoker's head. If a man believed his brand was special, then it was—at least to him. The mind is powerful like that, and Arturo Sr. knew it.

A BRIEF HISTORY OF CUBA

Cuba was basically blindsided by the collapse of the Soviet Union in December 1991. Up until 1991, the Cuban government was subsidized by the Soviets. The collapse of the Soviets was devastating to their economy and everything else. The Cubans were given vouchers for their weekly/monthly food rations. They might get some coffee, sugar, rice, and beans; their corner stores had almost nothing, and when I say nothing, I mean nothing. You might see one can of corn and a small box of powdered milk. There were diplomatic stores, but Cubans were not allowed to enter. Those were for foreigners only. I remember once seeing Cubans waiting outside asking people to buy stuff for them. It made me sad. We have it so good in the USA, but we don't know or appreciate it. We will one day know what we had when it's gone.

Cubans were also prohibited from eating beef. It was strictly for tourists, and it was a serious offense. They were also not allowed to buy or sell dollars. At one point, I had a friend who was sentenced to eight years in prison for buying and selling dollars. He would take a pack of cigarettes and empty all but one. He would empty all the tobacco and carefully roll the bills and slip them into the cigarette paper, add a little tobacco to the tip, and put them back into the box. He left the one full cigarette upside down. If the cops took a look, it all looked normal.

Cuba had come up with a pretty simple system to keep their eyes on everyone. They involved the people by turning everyone against each other and into snitches. First, they had a lot of cops on foot patrol just walking the neighborhood. They gave each cop an area of a few blocks that they were responsible for. Then they appointed a civilian in each block on each street to be the watchman or snitch. This person was mostly hated, but there was nothing anyone could do. Everything was reported, and these snitches took their jobs seriously. If someone arrived in a car to visit a resident, they filed a report; if you came home with someone, they filed a report, etc.

There was another phenomenon that took place—*la jinetera*, which means "prostitute," but a little different; it certainly felt different. I'll explain.

In the years after the Soviet influence in Cuba opened the doors to foreign tourism, in the beginning, it was mostly French Canadians, and this word originates with them. Later, the predominant horny tourists were the Spaniards; then came the Italians, followed by the Mexicans. As I have mentioned, Cubans had nothing, and people were desperate. The young women saw that the only real option was to get money from the tourists, by any means possible.

The young girls would come from all over the Cuban island, mostly to the Havana area. There was even a time when the government picked them up off the streets and checked IDs. If their *carnet* (personal federal ID) was from outside of Havana, they were locked up and sent home on a train. That didn't work very well, however, and for a period of time, they started shaving their heads and sending them home. At least that kept them away until their hair grew back.

These girls were attractive, mostly between the ages of twelve and twenty-two, wild, and having fun. Island life is very pleasant with warm, sunny days and long, warm nights. The girls didn't work at a brothel or stand on a specific corner. Instead, they just floated…they stood, walked, and wandered everywhere. We could be driving down Fifth Avenue and see the most beautiful girl and offer her a ride, but 99 percent of the time, she would get into the car and become part of our group, hang out, eat, and drink with us. Sometimes we would see a girl go around the block, and she was gone! There were guys all over the place, too, all foreigners from several different countries, mostly Europeans, all driving around having fun like kids in a candy store.

You know, it was almost magical—it really was. Something close to amazing for men, or for any man.

You could spend all day at the beach in Havana, hanging with your buddies, drinking, tanning, laughing, with no pressure. No ass-kissing. No arguments. No woman is grinding down your patience.

And at the end of the day—every day, if you wanted—you could meet a young, pretty girl who'd hop in your car and spend the next fourteen hours in a full-blown love affair. It didn't matter that it wasn't "real"—it felt real. And they felt amazing. Maybe for the only time in their lives, or maybe it just made them feel young again.

They were fucking and sucking at will. I watched so many guys live this out, and I always smiled. I got it. It felt great. That island, poor as it was, had something magical about it—the heat, the light, the rhythm. Almost-naked women shaking their stuff—literally—everywhere you turned. They weren't looking for love, but they could make any man feel like a king.

You didn't need to be rich or handsome. Just be you and ride the wave. Everyone—every tourist—was rich compared to a Cuban. That was the unspoken truth.

STREET TAXES

At the end of the trip, my two suitcases were packed. I had seventy boxes of real Cuban cigars that I bought in Cuba; no doubt about their origin. I traveled all the way here while on federal supervision and risked my freedom and my life to make some money. I wanted to move forward with my life, and this opportunity presented itself, so you better believe I jumped in headfirst.

So there I was in front of the Havana airport, about to walk into the unknown. We walked to the counter and registered; everything went smoothly and easily. The process wasn't fast; they did everything manually and were very careful not to let a Cuban national escape through the airport. Once we checked in, we had to line up for immigration. It was a wall of booths with no way to see what was beyond. I also went through the immigration process without issue. I then walked through the dark doorway and into the waiting area for departing passengers. It was a long process to get through, and we were now almost late for our flight. The airline was already calling our names. They knew we had checked in, but we hadn't yet boarded.

As I came out of the other side, there was a checkpoint, an X-ray machine, and customs agents; they made everyone run all of their bags and belongings through the machine. As I exited through the immigration gate and entered the waiting area, hearing my name poorly announced, I saw our two checked bags waiting there in the open, not just waiting but looking out of place and just wrong. I put sixty dollars (three twenty-dollar bills) inside my passport. I tried not to pay attention to the bags and hoped this was something normal. It wasn't.

I was now under pressure. My flight was close to departure, and customs now called my name over the intercom system. I was taken into a room by a small man, about five feet tall and 110 pounds, about thirty years old, and he had a serious look on his face. I pretended not to speak Spanish; I spoke English only. He was thrown off by my USA passport and that there was cash inside it.

He asked me a bunch of questions, and I showed him my receipts from Capi. We spoke some more, and he asked me why there was cash in my passport. I told him it was for him if he wanted it.

He froze and looked at me hard. Then a woman came into the private room and told him my plane would leave without me. He took the money and let me go.

I was flying high. As I came out of the room, Eduardo looked like he needed a diaper change. I smiled a bit and watched as the agents took my bags back inside, and we boarded a bus. At that time, there were no jetways, only buses that took everyone out to the runway to board via the stairs.

We flew from Havana to Mexico City, and our bags were checked in all the way back to GDL (Guadalajara Airport). At that time, the bags were tagged with an orange sticker letting everyone know that it's from an international connection. They also put the same tag on the carry-on bags. This way, the customs agents, cops, and federales can pick you out of a crowd. We finally landed in GDL about 7:00 p.m. that day. The top federal agent in charge of the GDL airport met me at the baggage claim and escorted me out of the airport. I gave him $250 ($125 per bag).

I was now home with my first load out of Cuba. My mind was

racing! I realized I had just made an important contact. The seventy boxes cost me about $1,500 plus expenses, but I gained so much info and experience.

FATE

I knew I needed to go directly back to Cuba. I believed I could find the same customs agent I'd met before, and that would give me the edge I needed to get all the cigars I wanted out of Cuba.

I was back on a plane two days later, GDL to Mexico City to Havana, alone.

While waiting for the plane to board in Mexico City, I ran into a Cuban guy I knew from GDL (Guadalajara), Elier; he was a real character. He was a hustler; he sold plastic bags to stores and shops in GDL and went back and forth to Cuba often. He brought fake Levi's jeans, fake Nikes, and gold-plated chains to Cuba. He was just now getting started with cigars.

He asked me if I would help him with some checked bags that he had. I asked what they contained, and he explained. I reluctantly agreed and told him not to talk to or acknowledge me. I said, "Just give me a sign when you see a bag you want me to pick up."

When we got to the bag area and the bags started coming out, I was quietly waiting and trying to blend in and be discreet. Then out of nowhere, Elier starts to yell "*Escot*" (that's how he said my name) and points at a huge duffel bag. Everyone within two miles saw and heard him. He did this two more times.

I now had a luggage cart piled with three huge, oversized duffel bags and my small personal bag.

I tried to maintain my composure and pretend it was all fine. As I approached the exit, I went to the "Green" (nothing to declare) side. When I got there, a female customs agent stopped me and asked me for my passport. I gave her the passport, and she led me into a private screening room and told me to wait. After a few moments, the door opened, and a male agent came in.

At that moment, he and I were both looking down, he at my passport and me at something to just act nonchalant. I was on one side of the table and he was on the other.

We both looked up at the same time, and to my delight, it was the same agent I was coming to search for, the same guy who had stopped me only three days ago. I had planned to stake out the terminal to hunt him down. I had traveled all the way to Havana alone, expecting to be waiting at the airport for maybe days until I saw and found him, and here he was.

It had to be fate; it all just came together on its own, and I was intoxicated. He didn't recognize me (he sees a lot of people each day), and he asked me if I had anything to declare. I said no. He asked if I was carrying anything for the Cuban guy, and I said yes. I told him of my relationship to the guy, and he told me they were watching him and knew he was smuggling contraband.

Then I said, "It's me, from the other day. I came here so fast just to find you."

He froze. He got really serious and closed the door to the room. "You lied to me," he said. "You pretended you didn't speak Spanish!"

I told him I was nervous and just didn't know how to act.

He then gave me his phone number on the smallest of papers, really small, like about a half-inch of paper. He told me to call him in five days. *Fuck, I have to sit idle for five days*, I thought. He also told me not to tell this to anyone and to stay away from the Cuban guy (Elier). He was being watched. I was allowed to leave the airport without incident, and they also let Elier leave because of me.

It was a smuggler's dream to have a contact in the Havana airport, but it wasn't easy.

I had time to wait, so I had Eduardo pick up the suitcases and fly to Havana to meet me. Once Eduardo was in Havana, I started visiting people and shopping for cigars. I hadn't yet bought any cigars at the factories or official stores. I was just getting my feet wet.

The days passed slowly, and I was going crazy. What was going to happen with this customs agent? Was he going to help me get my cigars out of Cuba? I wondered if I was wasting my time. *Why did he make me wait almost a week to meet?*

I called my contact on the fifth day at the time he told me. I was so impatient, I was just sitting around wasting time and spending money. I can't sit idle, even to this day, at fifty-eight years old. I can't sit still, I can't waste time, I need to be productive.

He set a place and time for the next day. We didn't say anything incriminating, only the place and time. Sunday at noon at a crappy little half-indoor, half-outdoor restaurant in the Guanabacoa area, about thirty minutes from central Havana. It's another place lost in time, old, unkept, lots of people walking aimlessly, and the lines for the "wowwow," the bus, can be as long as one block. Time isn't money in Cuba.

Eduardo came with me, and we took a street taxi (someone using their private car) to the place. There was my guy already sitting at a table. I like to arrive at these types of meetings early, more than an hour early, so I can get a feel, try to acclimate, and see if anything feels wrong. I have aborted meetings because of these "feelings" more than once in my life. He was already there too. We sat down, and we went through the formalities and chitchat. He then asked to have Eduardo please go to another area so we could "talk." Eduardo left, and we continued.

He asked me what I wanted. I was clear. I wanted to pay him to help me make sure to get my cigars out of the country without a problem. He asked me if they were store-bought cigars, and I assured him that they were. He went on to explain the problems that were starting with the "street" cigars and the pressure being put on them.

He was shaking and scared. I tried my best to make him feel at ease. We had a few beers and kept talking. He was worried about getting caught; he supported his wife and parents, his brother was a high-level doctor, and their lives were calm, very calm, and very poor. He made seven dollars a month.

He asked me several times about Eduardo and if he could be trusted. I told him I trusted him, but he was very nervous and uncomfortable. He told me Eduardo looked weak. I told him not to worry; we were solid and discreet. He then began to tell me about the secret police and a building they call *Todos Cantan*, "Everyone Sings." He said that it was a terrible place.

We finally got down to business. He said he personally had never worked with someone with cigars, but one of his coworkers (Diego) did, and he had already consulted him. He would have Diego handle it this time. He gave me Diego's work schedule. I had to go to the travel agency to pick a flight home that would be covered by one of his shifts.

He asked me how many boxes and how many suitcases. I still wasn't sure, but I said eight suitcases because I had three other guys with me and wanted to get the most bang for the buck.

It would cost me $150 per suitcase. I gave him $1,200 in payment.

We now all sat together and ate and drank. His name was Raul. He was very nervous, and I could tell he never really relaxed. He wasn't built for this stuff, but he was Cuban, and they know about adversity.

I felt like I drank a bottle of adrenaline! I had a lot of cigars in my room already packed up. I still didn't know much about choosing cigars or suitcases, but they were packed and ready to travel.

We arrived at the airport as indicated, and I was told to get there three hours before the flight. The drive from the city to the airport is thirty to forty minutes. It's a calm and simple drive. Once out of the city center, it becomes almost like the country. We saw remnants of the old, abandoned factories and farms along the way.

The airport was very small and not exciting. There just wasn't much tourism at this time. The outside area was always busy. I loved to watch the people as they tried to get something from someone, even selling cigars at the airport. I would enjoy watching the dynamics between the foreigners and the Cuban girls (I don't say "women" because they were all young). I could see disinterest in their eyes. The gaze, they were just doing a job and had no real interest at all; just a blank stare. Once I saw a girl, white, blond, maybe five foot ten, hugging a small man, maybe five foot two, dark skinned and chubby. He looked like he had died and gone to heaven, and she looked like she was dreaming about getting out of Cuba yesterday.

She waited and waved goodbye as he disappeared through the dark tunnel of immigration. She went over to the arrival area; the girls would just wait to see what foreigner they could meet on the next incoming flight.

We formed the line to get to the Mexicana Airlines counter to check in, and I had to be alert and organize everything and everyone. We got to the counter to check in, and from behind where the bags go on the moving belt came an official wearing his green military clothing. He took a stool at the counter and started checking out documents. Then he asked me how many bags I had. I told him eight. He was a white guy and could pass for almost any ethnicity with his blue eyes and curly blond hair.

This was Diego. He was smooth, calm, had self-confidence, and was in control. Behind the wall where all the luggage went were several X-ray machines that 100 percent of all bags had to pass through. Agents were watching everything.

He was very easy to deal with, was good at what he did, and I knew him and he knew me. We were checked in and went through immigration and security without issue. This time, my bags were not out in the open waiting for me. We boarded our plane for home. Again, our plane landed in Mexico City, and we ran for our connecting flight to Guadalajara.

Once in GDL, we were met by the top cop of the airport. His guys even helped carry my bags outside to the parking lot. I paid them $1,000 for their service.

It wasn't cheap, but now I had my connection in both Mexican and Cuban customs.

SLICK BERNY

Along comes Berny.

He was introduced to me by Howard Frum. The guy talked a big game and said he could sell thousands of boxes. But everyone in the cigar world knew Berny was a mooch. He was in his early sixties but acted like he was twenty-five. Mr. Smooth. He thought he was slick.

To be fair, he tried to help me out, but nobody took him seriously. They didn't want him around, and by extension, they didn't want me around either—guilt by association. I tried to ditch him, but he was like gum on the bottom of your shoe. He just stuck.

So I made a deal. I gave him my last fourteen boxes. I told him if he could move some product—more than he smoked—I'd consider giving him more. I made it clear that someone would call him to collect, and he was to pay as he sold.

Truth was, I was tired. Tired of hustling, tired of chasing sales. I just wanted to get back to Mexico. Summer was creeping up on Chicago, and I was ready to go.

I warned Berny what would happen if he fucked me.

He fucked me anyway.

He dodged calls, gave Stuart the runaround, lied, and ghosted. I finally got fed up and lit into him. I told him to stop screwing around and pay me like he said he would. Still, the same story. No answers. More bullshit.

On that same trip, just before leaving town, I squared up with a longtime friend I owed some money to. It was for a deal I didn't agree with, but business is business. I called him and offered cigars as payment. I had saved six good boxes for him. I told him to meet me at O'Hare, International Terminal 5, as I was checking in. He was happy to take them, and he thought he was getting a great deal. Maybe we both won.

I kept calling Berny. On our last call, I told him, "Don't piss me off, or I'll handle it differently." His response? "We can throw down, if you want, whatever you want."

I reminded him I was two thousand miles away, but only one short flight from being right back in front of him. I wasn't gone—just away for a moment.

I hung up smiling, shaking my head. So many guys are just plain stupid. Doing business, especially in the streets, is hard. Dealing with people is harder.

But I didn't want to act until I spoke to Howard. I owed Howard a lot. If he told me to forgive Berny, I would've. Simple as that.

And yeah—maybe fourteen boxes doesn't sound like much. But to me, that was close to $5,000. In the street, guys have been killed for fifty bucks. It wasn't just about the money. It was the principle. Getting burned sucks, and I hated the feeling. Especially when I was busting my ass just to get these cigars here. This is far from the end of Berny…

Every penny counted. I didn't want to screw anyone. But I wasn't going to let anyone screw me either. But before I hit the streets, I had unfinished business.

Berny.

I had given him cigars on consignment, and he hadn't paid. He thought he could skate by, maybe pretend it didn't matter. What he didn't realize was that I came from a place where disrespect has consequences.

I went to see Howard Frum.

Howard ran a jewelry store downtown. I'd bought my first Rolex from him in 1984—a gold President with a white face. Howard knew who I was. He'd seen me come up. He'd always treated me with respect. He was loud, funny, and one of those sharp-tongued Jewish guys who yelled during business but never held a grudge.

I told him what happened with Berny.

Howard picked up the phone and called him right in front of me. Started yelling. Cursing. Telling Berny he was a moron for messing with me. "Don't fuck with Scott," he said. "He's the real deal—kick-boxer, street guy; he'll hang you out a window by your feet."

Berny, of course, played tough guy. He always did. Howard hung up on him and turned to me.

"Fuck him," he said. "He's got a Rolex I sold him. Take it from him. I'll buy it back from you."

That's old-school.

Howard did me a favor. He stuck up for me. So I went to him first out of respect. That's how I was raised. You don't forget who does right by you. Favors get paid back in kind—not with money, but with loyalty.

That's how the game is played where I come from.

SURPRISE, SURPRISE

Remember, Berny owed me money—almost five grand—and he was jerking me around, acting tough. I warned him once, then I told him flat out, "Don't fuck with me." I wasn't dragging bags and boxes of cigars across countries just to get played. This was hard, dirty work, and I wasn't letting anyone get one over on me.

It was a warm summer day when I showed up at Berny's place. He lived on the second floor of a two-flat that looked like a house from the outside. The neighborhood was lower-middle class, mid-gentrification. Some blocks had fresh paint and new windows; others were still frozen in time.

I brought Stu and Wacker with me.

Stu was six feet, 200 pounds, but Wacker was a whole different animal—a six foot four, 250-pound thug, prison tattoos on both arms, wearing a white ribbed tank top before they were cool. The guy looked like trouble even when he was smiling.

I rang the doorbell. Berny's wife answered. She said he wasn't home but invited us in to wait. Perfect.

The apartment was small and modest. We were left in the front room—couch, a little desk, a humidor on a table near us. That humidor said it all. Berny didn't have money, but he wanted the image—Rolex, cigars, and pretending he was part of the lifestyle. I scanned the place for anything else of value, just in case this turned into a collection visit.

About ten minutes later, Berny walked in, and he wasn't happy to see me.

Right away, he started with excuses. The cigars were bad. They were old. They weren't fresh. Maybe they were fakes. I listened and calmly said, "Then give them back. Simple." But more excuses came. I started getting hot.

Then he says he's calling Howard.

"What the fuck does Howard have to do with what you owe me?" I snapped. "Give me the cigars, and I'll be on my way."

He told me to get out of his house and said he'd pay me once his people paid him.

That was it.

He reached for the phone, and I exploded over the couch. I almost kicked Stu in the face and grabbed Berny by the neck. I wrapped one arm around his and gripped his throat with the other. The momentum slammed us both into the entrance door with a loud, echoing bang. His head hit hard.

The cockiness disappeared.

I said, "Give me the fuckin' watch until you've got my money, then I'll give it back."

He told me he didn't have it.

"Wacker," I barked, "search the house."

By now, both Wacker and Stu were locked in. Probably surprised at how fast things escalated. I was past the point of talking.

I dragged Berny about ten feet to a side window and told him I was about to throw him out upside down.

He wasn't taking me seriously, like no one had ever actually put hands on him before. Just another poser who thought playing tough was the same as being tough.

I reached my limit and slapped him—hard. Not a punch. Just enough to snap him to attention without knocking him out.

That lit the fuse.

Wacker and Stu jumped in. We had him 70 percent out the window, legs in the air, head dangling, when his wife rushed in offering us the watch.

She was calm. Too calm. Like she knew the drill. She held it out the way you'd feed a stray dog that might bite your hand. "Just take the stupid watch," she said.

We pulled him inside, dropped Berny to the floor, grabbed the watch, and walked out in single file.

Our car was parked about a block away. Once we were clear of the building, we picked up the pace. There was always a chance they'd call the cops. That's never good. The whole time I sold cigars, I never once gave anyone my last name. Just "Scott" or "Scott Anthony."

I went straight to Howard's shop.

The second I walked in, he lit up.

"What the fuck did you do to Berny, Scott?" he shouted. "You hung him out a window? You slapped him? Took his Rolex? In his own fuckin' house?"

I just looked at him. "You told me to do it."

"Yeah, but I didn't think you'd actually do it!" He laughed.

I told him the story—just the facts. One slap. No blood. No bones broken.

He shook his head, grinning. "You're crazy."

We had a good laugh. I handed him the Rolex. He handed me what Berny owed.

I never heard from Berny again.

LOOKS COUNT

I had a pretty good assortment of cigars stored and waited for my next trip. I got home and thought, *I'm not going to take a trip to the border for a few weeks. How should I take care of the cigars?* You see, Cuba not only grows the tobacco and manufactures a great cigar, but the climate and the high humidity are the best for the integrity of the cigars themselves.

I had to accept it: looks do count. It was a hard pill to swallow, but I had to do it, even though it would mean a lot more work for me.

I'm now thinking about how to preserve this and make sure I won't have customers complaining again. The last few sales trips to Chicago had been riddled with issues. I finally paid attention to the boxes and understood why people cared. They were judging a book by its cover.

The boxes would rub together during the thousands of arduous miles they traveled. This would produce rub marks, scuffs, dings, dents, scratches, and could even cause the boxes to break or collapse, and they just looked bad. These customers were paying up to $1,200 for a box; they lived in large, nice homes, drove nice cars, and kept them up well. They were people who had their shit together.

Who wants to buy an exclusive, high-end product that looks like shit?

I know the simple truth is that the box doesn't matter as far as the cigar goes. The boxes mostly end up in the trash or as a kid's toy. But it's all about the eyes and mind. I knew I had to change my care for the cigars as well as the boxes. I didn't want to have to deal with unsatisfied customers anymore. It was already a big headache. I had lost a few sales because of these issues and had a lot of comments and complaints.

I had a closet under a set of stairs on the bottom floor of the gym. It was a room I used for martial arts classes, and I had my equipment stored in this closet: boxing gloves, focus mitts, jump ropes, and all that. I had even built wood shelves to store the equipment. I removed all the equipment and stored it away. I then cleaned the room very well, several times. I went to a high-end store that had a large tobacco section, because I was looking for a humidity meter (hygrometer). I found a simple, gold-colored meter for a few bucks. I took it back to the room and placed it where I could easily see it when I opened the door.

I opened the door the next day, and the meter was 70 percent. The room was perfect! I had already left all the suitcases inside the small room, and now I emptied them all neatly into the room. The room couldn't have been more perfect. I organized all my boxes on the shelves, and they were well-placed and organized. It looked amazing, and all the colors of the different boxes perfectly lined up like a cigar store or warehouse.

The room wasn't even close to full; I could fit probably three times as many cigars in my new "walk-in humidor." It was in the back corner of the room and didn't attract any attention. The only detail was that I only felt comfortable "working" there when the gym was closed, after 11:00 p.m., or on weekend evenings. This is when I could leave the door open and work freely.

It felt good, and I felt proud. I had my very own walk-in humidor, and it didn't cost me anything.

Now it was time to think about how to keep the cigars in good condition while they were traveling.

I came up with an idea. I went to a packing supply store and bought a batch of small plastic bags and rolls of plastic wrap. I then went to the pharmacy and bought a jumbo bag of cotton balls.

I filled a large bowl with water and started by wetting the bottom of each of the wooden cigar boxes with a sponge. This first step would help a lot, since the water would soak into the wood a little and keep a natural humidity in the package too.

Then I would take a cotton ball, wet it, and put one or two into each little bag. I would prepare about one hundred of these and have them ready for the process. First, I would take the cigar box with the wet bottom, put one of the plastic bags on the top, and wrap the plastic around as I would add the second little bag with the wet cotton balls, and then proceed to wrap the whole box. This would allow the boxes to keep their humidity and also protect them from damage.

This was a lot of work. For one hundred boxes, it would take a few hours. I would do it late at night, alone, and in a quiet room. I would start to do it a few days before I left for the border.

It was still early in the cigar craze, but it was becoming more popular by the day, and that meant more people were interested in getting involved. I wasn't interested in just taking a few trips to Cuba and making a few bucks. It was all or nothing. I had only a handful of customers so far, and I didn't want to lose any; I wanted more. But I knew it was not going to be simple. I could already tell that most of the people who smoked cigars were going to be successful men. These are the kind of guys who want the best.

I was going to get them what they wanted. I would find the best cigars (I still needed to learn) with brand-new-looking boxes.

Chapter Five

MCALLEN

I WAS TIRED OF THE PROBLEMS AT THE NOGALES BORDER
crossing and decided to try another route. I spoke to Mario "Azabache" and Oscar, and we decided to take the bus to Reynosa, Mexico. Reynosa is the Mexican border town near McAllen, Texas.

I opened my cigar closet one night about midnight, and I worked until about 6:00 a.m. I wrapped and prepared 150 boxes of cigars. I didn't want to take too many on a new route, and it was really a test run. Each box would have the bottom moistened, a small plastic bag with wet cotton added, and then be tightly wrapped with commercial plastic wrap. It was almost perfect; it worked so well. I then prepared and packed the suitcases. Once they were prepared, I put them back into the closet/humidor until I was ready to leave.

The bus tickets to the border were about a hundred dollars per person. There were four of us when we left: me and Oscar, and Mario and Carlos, both active professional boxers on their way to train and suck some money out of a "businessman" in McAllen. I, of course, paid for everything for everyone: food, travel, and lodging.

We arrived in McAllen around noon, but we didn't have anyone we could trust, so Mario planned to introduce me to Ramiro. We got to a small, crappy hotel, fifteen dollars per night. Mario tried to find Ramiro, but he wasn't responding. We looked and looked with no luck. Again, I found myself in a shithole border town with a bunch of suitcases full of cigars, stuck and alone.

Somehow Ramiro found us. He came to our room, and we finally met. He gave me a completely different "vibe" than other scumbag smuggler who had been to our room earlier. He was a young guy, twenty-two-ish, short, and stocky. He was well-known by the "businessmen" Mario had been staying with, and he was recommended. He told me what hotel to stay in on the USA side, and said he would bring all the bags to my room in the early morning hours the next day. We loaded all the bags into his white Chevy pickup truck, and he drove away. What a feeling of relief. I'd finally found him, and he was cool.

We already had the room paid for and were planning to stay on the Mexican side for the night, so we went back to the room. All four of us were in the room with only two double beds. I was in one bed, and Mario and Carlos were in the other. Oscar was standing, reading something from a book. The room door was open, but the screen door was closed, because it was hot and muggy.

We were focused on the TV when out of nowhere, the room was rushed by federales!

We were overwhelmed immediately. The look on their faces was priceless, really priceless. None of us even blinked; we just sat there watching TV. There were no bags. Earlier that day when we couldn't find our main guy Ramiro, Oscar went out to the streets and came back with another guy who did the same work (crossing product) but he gave me a bad vibe. It was an event at the hotel, that's for sure. The parking lot had more than ten cars of agents, and it was loud. Finally, the "comandante" came in, looked around the obvious shithole, and saw nothing. We all had our own small bags, and those were searched quickly, but that was it. All the other bags were gone.

It never hurt to have Mario "Azabache" Martinez with me. He

was famous and loved in Mexico. He had fought for the world title many times and had more than sixty professional fights. He turned pro at the ripe age of fourteen years old. He fought Azumah Nelson twice, Jeff Fenech, and Roger Mayweather. He also had a famous fight with Julio Cesar Chavez in 1984 when he was just nineteen years old.

I talked to the boss inside the room. He said, "Okay, where's the drugs? I know you guys had drugs."

I laughed and assured him they were only cigars. We slowly made our way outside, and I noticed the scale of what was happening. He had thirty guys with him. It was a catch-22 for him because we didn't have anything, and we were not doing anything wrong. But he was in charge and could do anything he wanted to us if he really wanted to.

We spoke for a few minutes, and he started dispatching his guys. He then told me straight out, "I didn't come here to waste my time, and I'm not leaving with an empty hand." He went back and forth for about fifteen minutes (it felt like hours), and I gave him $400 for his troubles. Then he was gone as quickly as he appeared.

The next day, we got a ride across the bridge to the other side, the USA. I went to the McAllen airport to rent a car and went to the motel where Ramiro told me to stay. It was outside of the city and kind of all alone on a road outside of town. Since the border stretches forever, we were near the border and near the point where Ramiro and his crew of guys did their crossing. There was nothing within walking distance and nothing within sight either. It was a small, 1970s-looking, one-story motel that looked more like a garage than a motel.

On one occasion, I went out for a jog. When I got back to the room, I got down on the floor to do pushups. When I was in the down position, with my face close to the floor, I saw that the carpet was loaded with marijuana. There were weed trimmings, shake, seeds, all of it. This hotel was probably used by so many people after crossing their drugs across the river; they needed a place to repack.

The following morning at approximately 5:00 a.m., I was woken by pounding on my door. I jumped up and asked, "Who?"

"*Soy yo Weto!*"

I opened the door. Ramiro was there with a car backed up to the front of my door. He had a few guys with him, and they started unloading and passing the bags to me, one at a time. I would turn around and toss each one into my room. I gave him $1,200 then and there, and they got back into the car and drove off. I stayed up for about another hour, peeking through the curtains and making sure everything was clear and okay. Then I went back to sleep for a few hours. When I woke up, I had a whole new dilemma.

These border towns are isolated from the rest of civilization, and there is really only one or two roads out, and they are heavily patrolled by so many different police. This increases the probability that you'll get stopped, and it's almost a guarantee that if you get stopped, you'll get searched. Even though it's not really permitted by the constitution, the police do as they please most of the time.

The roads out of the Valley are like a video game to the cops; they catch so many people moving drugs every day.

I really felt stuck. I wasn't yet sure what to do.

I went to a few local cigar shops. I was just looking and thinking. I tried to strike up a conversation, but it wasn't easy. The people in these small towns don't really trust outsiders, since there are so many drug deals and all that. They just don't accept people easily.

At the last store I went to, I saw the UPS truck pull up and unload boxes for the cigar store. I noticed they had some open boxes in the area and were unloading cigar boxes. Flash, the light bulb went off, and I thought, *We are all the way down in the middle of nowhere, and almost everything needs to be shipped here or shipped out. It shouldn't look suspicious if I shipped a few cardboard boxes of cigars, right?*

I drove to the UPS office and took a look. It was normal, with no visible police or security, and a lot of people coming and going. I asked about boxes, and they showed me their crappy, expensive boxes and tape. It was way overpriced and of poor quality. I came up with another idea.

I remembered seeing a few warehouse areas near my motel, so I decided to drive around there to look for boxes. One of the warehouses had the large overhead door open, and I could see that the warehouse was loaded with boxes. I went around the back, but there weren't any boxes, so I decided to go inside and ask. They were Chinese and spoke very little English, but they understood "free" boxes. They made a hand gesture over to an area where they had empty boxes. I started rummaging through the pile and chose what I calculated was enough.

I picked the ones that were thick, heavy-duty cardboard; they were much more sturdy than the cheap ones that are sold at packing stores. Plus, they were free! I packed them one inside of the other, so it didn't take as much space in the car, and I didn't want to bother these people any more than I already did, so I wanted to make only one trip out. I thanked them and left. I loaded the back seat of the car and drove off. I then went to Home Depot to get some heavy-duty tape; all of this would have cost me fifty bucks or more at the UPS place, and it probably only cost me $4.99, plus the quality wasn't even comparable.

Back at the motel, I unloaded the boxes into the room and started packing them. If there was any space left over, I tore the extra boxes into pieces and used the dense cardboard to fill the space. I didn't want to have any wiggle room. I wanted them to be tight and solid to give them overall support. This helped a lot with the boxes wrapped in plastic because the plastic made them more complicated to pack, but they stuck together once in place, and this protected them too.

I knew the importance of preserving the integrity and aesthetics of the boxes, so it was now a priority. I didn't want the thin, single-layer cardboard boxes, because they tear and smash easily.

I didn't tape the boxes closed in my room, because when I was in the UPS office, I saw that they asked a few people what was inside, and they kind of scrutinized a little. So I loaded the car with my boxes. I had boxes everywhere: back seat, front seat, and in the trunk. I got to the UPS office and purposely made myself seen, heard, and noticed.

I thought it would be best if I acted like, well, basically like an idiot. So I started unloading boxes from the car and carried them into the building, where I was making a work area for myself. I spoke to the counter people and asked a few questions. I had all the boxes open and started taping them right there out in the open. I even asked an employee to help me hold the flap closed as I taped it; they surely saw the cigar boxes. It would be almost impossible for them to distinguish that their origin was Cuba.

I then went through the entire process of filling out all the labels and papers, and when they asked what I was shipping, I simply said, "Cigars." They didn't even blink. I sent the boxes to my mother's apartment, where she now lived, about thirty minutes outside the city of Chicago.

I had taken care of the cigars, but I was now kind of stranded in McAllen, Texas. I started looking for a way to get back to Chicago. At this time, there was no real internet, so I had to call airline after airline to check prices. A place like McAllen or Laredo has small airports, and they're located at the end of the line. You don't find cheap fares to or from these places. I was able to get a decent flight out of Houston, Texas, so now I had to get to Houston. I returned the rental car to the airport and got a Greyhound bus to Houston. It was more than a seven-hour ride to Houston, but I wasn't in a hurry; I was told the boxes would take about four days to arrive. I had sent them ground; this was cheaper and less scrutinized.

The bus was searched at least three times after we left the bus station. I'm sure the bags were also searched at the bus station in McAllen. You have the border patrol looking for illegals and the customs looking for drugs. I learned to avoid this route in the future.

I eventually got to my mother's house and had to wait a few days. I made phone calls to track the packages. I was uneasy. I didn't know if they would make it or not; I had to just cross my fingers and trust the odds. The odds are that all boxes are searched in some way, coming from anywhere near the border, most likely by X-ray machines and drug-sniffing dogs. I was like a lion in a cage while waiting for UPS to arrive. I couldn't really leave the house because I needed to be there when they arrived.

My mother lived in a condo building, three stories, middle-class, with mostly middle-aged people. She lived on the third floor with her balcony facing the front of the building. I probably looked out the window for the UPS truck two hundred times over those few days.

When the truck arrived, I scanned the parking lot and the entire area. I didn't see anyone or anything that looked out of place.

I went down to the front door of the lobby to meet the driver; he, too, was calm and normal. I piled my boxes into the lobby and made a few trips to get them upstairs. Once upstairs, I immediately started calling customers. At this point, I only had a handful of customers, and I called them all. I then opened the boxes and unloaded them all onto the living room floor of my mother's apartment. I loaded each duffel bag with a variety of cigars. Some customers liked only certain brands and sizes, and others would choose by price. Many would buy the cigars as gifts, and others followed the recommendations from *Cigar Aficionado* magazine.

The next day, I had my appointment with my federal probation officer. I took my car, the trunk loaded with two hundred boxes of cigars, and I drove to his office. Oscar waited for me in the car while I went in for my appointment. Remember, I had to do this about every four to six weeks; it was supposed to be monthly, but I had managed to stretch it a few more weeks.

Here I was in his office talking to him, and the whole time I've got a trunk full of Cuban cigars for sale. He was a very cool guy, and even though it was many years ago, I feel bad about it. But not bad enough to tell him about it.

From there, I went to Howard's, and I could finally get back to selling again.

HOWARD FRUM AND OSCAR

Normally, Howard greeted me with that easy smile and a warm welcome, but not this time. Before I was even through the door, before it had fully closed behind me, he hit me with it:

"Hey, one of my guys has a problem with some cigars you sold him."

Just like that. No hello. No small talk. Just straight into it. I froze.

"Who? What? When?"

He told me it was my guy—someone who came to him saying he had cigars from me. And my guy turned out to be Oscar.

Apparently, Oscar had brought in his own boxes of Cohiba Espléndidos—the solid wood ones—and they were bad. Really bad. The customer had reached out to Howard, pissed, thinking they were mine.

That kind of thing causes collateral damage—always. Bad cigars meant bad press. I had just started with this client, and he could've become something. Not a major buyer—he only bought a few boxes at a time—but I needed everyone I could get.

And just like that, Oscar fucked it up. I left Howard's place fuming. Burning inside.

I started calling around. Looking for him. That little fucker was already in town and hadn't even told me he was here. And not only that, but he was trying to do what I did—sneaking around, selling cigars, going directly to my contacts behind my back.

This is exactly why guys get murdered in Mexico, or in the drug world in general. Everyone's always trying to fuck each other over.

I was done. Fed up. Boiling. When I finally tracked him down, I didn't even hold back.

I sat right in front of him and said, "What the fuck, Oscar? Your business is other crap, not cigars. Why would you do this to me? You went to my friend. You told him those boxes were mine, and they were garbage."

He just stared at me, confused, tilting his head like a dumb dog. It was unreal. He couldn't even grasp why I was angry.

He tried to wiggle out of it, telling me he bought the boxes from some Cuban guy in Guadalajara. By the time he got to Tucson, they were scratched up and looked like shit. So what did he do?

He sanded the boxes.

Then he varnished them with the cigars still inside.

I couldn't believe what I was hearing. Cigars are like sponges. They absorb everything—especially chemicals. His cigars were ruined. They tasted like varnish and smelled like furniture polish. And beyond that, they were just junk. An inferior product.

That's when I knew it was over. Not kill him over. But I needed to cut Oscar out of my life.

Sure, he was funny. Good company sometimes. Had a sharp mind. Could recite movie quotes like a human jukebox. But he wasn't loyal. And he always betrayed me when it counted.

This is exactly why I gave that speech to everyone I ever took with me, and why I never brought Oscar to Cuba.

He would've broken every rule and stuck it straight in my back.

MASTER CLASS

One night, about midnight, I got a call from the well-known "Chicago cigar guy." Mark Farrow was about forty-five years old, tall with a full head of graying hair. He told me that Howard Frum gave him my number. He invited me over to his apartment. He lived in a high-rise building in front of the lake and Lake Shore Drive in a very nice area of Chicago. I brought a lot of bags of cigars, at least fifty boxes. We got to know each other for a while, and we traded a lot of Cuba stories. We had a lot to talk about and compare.

I was about to get one of my first master classes in cigars.

Mark was surprised to see I had so many boxes. He had been hearing about me, but he didn't imagine the volume. Mark had been traveling to Cuba for about a year and would fly home from Canada with his cigars, maybe twenty-five boxes a trip. He also had a network of people who went and brought back some cigars, too, and he would buy them all. He just couldn't get enough and was always looking, as was I.

He started inspecting my boxes, and he was quick to notice the faults and imperfections, but he wasn't as concerned with the box as he was with the cigars themselves.

He would pull out two or three cigars from a box and use a toothpick to make small holes in the bottom and suck. This way, you could tell if the cigar will pull and ultimately smoke or be too tight and plugged. He told me I needed to learn how to pick and check the cigars.

You see, many details go into each cigar: the bands, ribbons, boxes, labels, seals, nails, dividers, spacers, color coding, rubber stamps, and stickers. This is always done best in the factories. They are the legitimate manufacturer of each brand. They market them as every company markets its product to as many people as possible. Most of the many people selling on the "street" don't care one bit about any of that; they sell whatever they can to make a buck and have a little better life. There are only a few who understand the importance of the quality and details.

So yes, factory cigars are pretty much a 100 percent guarantee that they will be the way they are supposed to be.

We got along well. Mark bought thirty boxes from me. He had some knowledge, that's for sure.

He went over the boxes like a jeweler examining precious stones. He chose the ones that were acceptable to him and were easier to sell. I was learning, too, that it wasn't just Cuban cigars that were in style; it was the idea, the lifestyle, the aura of Cuba, Fidel, and Che Guevara.

THE WALKING DEAD

There was one goal for most young Cubans at that time: to get out of Cuba, any way possible. They couldn't just get on a plane like I did. If they had contact with foreigners, they would use that route, befriend them, and try to get help to get out. Marriage was the most popular way to get out, so many girls got out this way and broke a lot of hearts around the world.

There was a real urgency for these people to get out…it was a desperation that no one can understand unless they were put under those same conditions. The women were very good at it; they played the game well. They were coy and modest, and men fell into their traps all the time. Young, beautiful Cuban women were leaving in large numbers and were going to countries around the world. These men were all in, but the girls usually left them immediately upon arrival at their destination.

There was a young boy who lived across the street from my hotel, in a dilapidated concoction that was a blend of living quarters. One day, he came over and started talking to us on the front steps of the hotel. It was just chitchat and joking around, but then it changed. It got sad, for me, anyway. The boy said he could always spot a Cuban citizen; he could immediately spot a foreigner too.

I challenged him. I said, "Come on, you can't tell. You may think you can, but you can't."

He was just a kid, maybe thirteen or fourteen years old. He was skinny, had a deep, dark tan, and his wild straight hair was bleached from the sun. He looked like an American kid from Florida.

He looked me right in the eyes and said, "When I look in your eyes, I see life, hope, the future. When I look in the eyes of any Cuban, I can see emptiness, no hope, just hunger."

It was profound because this young boy understood. He was right; there is a big difference. It was accurate; you could see a blank stare on most Cuban people. I was sad, and to this day, it makes me feel down just to think about it.

I would often notice and comment to people about this bizarre feeling in Cuba. In the early evening, when people were moving around from their jobs and lives to their homes, they were just like the walking dead.

It's an exaggeration for me to compare them to zombies, but the feeling was ominous. They were just in motion, no joy, no expression, just alive, with an empty stare. People didn't use words like "Thank you" and "Excuse me." If they bumped into you, they simply continued on their path. They were taught at one time that everyone is the same, no one is superior, so you don't need to ask for permission or apologize.

I also met a couple of guys who lived down the street from the hotel, about half a block toward the ocean/Malecón. They were usually outside sitting and doing nothing. These were the typical kids from the other side of the tracks; they were bust-outs and lost. They weren't tall in stature and were both thin; almost everyone in Cuba was thin at this time. There wasn't much to eat, and very little junk food. One was very dark skinned but not black, and he had a big mop of curly black hair. He was a little thicker than the other. The other was light-skinned and had his curly black hair tighter and groomed; he had refined facial features and was more thin.

They were always trying to talk to us and get something. I talked to them and sometimes would get them beer from the gas station down the street, across from the Melia Cohiba. We would sit on their stoop and smoke cigars and talk shit. These guys were poor with no hope in sight. They tried to offer me cigars, but it was always a waste of time. They had brought me to several different people to take a look, but it was always a dud.

But I kept going with them because one thing I learned is you never really know. You never know what you'll see or the contact you might make, especially in Cuba.

A NEW BIBLE

Meanwhile, in the USA, people are going nuts over cigars. There are whole magazines dedicated to cigars, with Cuban cigars at the top of the list.

I bought my first *Cigar Aficionado* magazine right before my first cigar buy. To me, it was the first step to educating myself about cigars. Before selling the cigars, the only experience I'd ever had with cigars was from my Uncle Joe. He always had a cigar hanging out of his mouth. He had a special way of talking. You speak a little differently when you have a cigar in your mouth. My Uncle Joe had Mob connections or was involved in the Chicago "Outfit," the Mafia. He was as Italian as you would find, and he was the family "fixer." I remember wishing he were around to help me, because he could have sold all my cigars, I'm sure.

I used *Cigar Aficionado* magazine for my benefit for the rest of my cigar days. I watched the magazine grow from a few pages to almost an inch thick. In every edition, they rated cigars, and the Cubans were almost always, if not always, the top-rated, and this really helped sometimes. Once I knew which ones rated high, I knew I could sell those fast and furiously. They ranked and rated, and they did this all the time.

They also did a lot of articles and pumped up the image of Cuba and Cuban cigars. Most guys who were smoking were never going to go to Cuba, never, so all they had was their imagination and *Cigar Aficionado* magazine.

I must have read that first issue I bought one hundred times. It was like a new bible for me. Its cover had Fidel Castro, summer 1994. I thought I was learning, but what was really happening was that I was being brainwashed.

They had a rating system for cigars, one hundred being the highest. The description of the cigars was so sexy and enticing: "The Punch Double Corona starts with a low flame…as it begins its first burn, you can taste the pine trees in the air…as it burns, you can smell the slight aroma of hickory in the air…as the cigar slowly burns toward the middle, there is a romantic taste of fine coffee…"

For a moment, I almost bought into it. It's all bullshit! I'm sure the magazine was corrupt as hell. They were making deals to give certain brands a plug, that's all. But it was worth it because I found out what cigars were popular and what would sell.

A TWO-YEAR DEGREE IN ONE DAY

On one trip, we didn't have our flight until the late evening, so we decided to have the driver take us to the Partigás cigar factory for the tour. The factory is in Havana, right behind the Capitol building. The rest of the neighborhood was falling, literally. We were dropped off near the front doors and were approached by at least eight different guys offering their cigars. But I was there for the tour. I wanted to learn and to see.

We went through the entire building and were shown and told about the entire process. We could ask questions, and these people here knew all the answers. I loved the tour. I definitely had a new level of cigar knowledge once the tour was over. All those details helped me in my cigar business and transactions.

I would eventually take that same tour four more times. I even befriended Papito, a master-level roller from the factory. He made Double Coronas all day long, six days a week, for his entire existence. He will never do anything more or different.

His wife also worked there, and they were given or allowed to have two cigars each per day. So each worker could take two cigars home per day, in their hand as they walked out, so they are in plain sight for the security officers to see. They could also take advantage and do this same process a few times a day instead of just quitting time, and they could also tell their coworkers that they would buy their cigars too. Soon, they could accumulate a nice quantity of fine cigars at a very discounted rate.

That way, they could start to live life just a little bit better.

You enter the factory through its Cigar Store. It's an old-world cigar shop with a rum and coffee bar, the aroma of cigar smoke permeating the air. Glass cases and glass-walled shelves were stocked with some of the finest cigars available in the world. But I didn't just see the cigars. I also noticed the pristine appearance of the boxes. That came in handy later.

In the first stage of the factory, there are bales of all kinds of tobacco from all over the island. Then they have the areas where they open, classify, and separate the leaves. You have huge open rooms filled with rollers from all sides. They are all sitting at their cigar roller workstations, diligently putting together their tobacco blend, preparing the roll, filling the molds, pressing the molds, opening the molds, cutting the rough edges, and finally applying the finishing cosmetic wrapper.

They then leave them in the waiting area, where they will be picked up by the person who pushes this cart around the factory all day, every day. This person picks up cigars from all the rollers, and they get mixed into the same place as all the others. They are then put into a room where they are separated by size and tone color, then they are transferred into the adjacent room where they are boxed according to the order they are filling.

They have so many different brands being rolled and boxed in the same place. How could there be any difference from brand to brand? Just another reminder that a cigar is a cigar, period. The difference is in the person's mind, 100 percent.

There was also a person on a stage at a podium giving live news reports. I don't remember what this person was called, but it's a tradition in all the factories. The workers had to be brainwashed while they were working.

To me, the tour was like a two-year degree all in one day. I really needed it, and I got what I needed. I was learning fast, and I became consumed with cigars. It was becoming especially important now to have my product correct and of high quality. I even wanted the boxes to be pristine. I needed the correct rubber stamps on the bottom of the boxes, the correct ribbons, the correct everything, down to the last detail.

The stamps on the bottom of the box identified the factory and the date of production; they were usually letters and numbers codes. The ribbons sometimes had the brand imprint on them; sometimes the street guys would use an incorrect ribbon and just turn it around so the customer wouldn't see it, but it eventually would get discovered. It happened to me more than once. It was a terrible feeling to get "busted" by a customer with something like this. I did everything I could to avoid it.

I eventually had a few guys out there who got me different items, parts if you will, like the bands and some papers, that kind of thing. I was always open to taking a look, because you never really knew who would have something interesting or worthwhile. Since these guys ran the streets around the factory, they had access to products and employees. They had a pretty amazing network of people all doing the same thing: making a buck and surviving.

Chapter Six

HARD LABOR

ONCE I GOT THE CIGARS INTO MEXICO FROM CUBA, I HAD TO find a way to get them over the border to the US. Every one of these trips was like a marathon for me: they were "fast and furious," not much food, and not much rest.

GOLDBERG

Erwin Goldberg was the general manager of the Toyota dealership where my childhood friend Stuart worked as a salesman. It had that Jewish mafia feel—not in the criminal sense, but the community sense. The owner, Gary, was the son of the founder, and like most of the staff, he was Jewish. They took care of their own. Loyalty ran deep in that place.

Erwin was about six feet one and maybe 125 pounds soaking wet. Sharp guy. Always cool with me. He gave me respect, and I returned it. His office was his house, and I treated it like that.

One day, we were sitting together, shooting the shit like we often did. He, like so many others, loved hearing my stories—the action, the chaos, the close calls. I could tell stories for hours, and they'd just sit there, shaking their heads in disbelief.

That day, Erwin leaned back in his chair, looked at me hard, and said, "There's got to be another way. Fuck, Scott. How do you keep dealing with this over and over?"

That line stuck with me.

"There's got to be another way."

I still say it out loud when things get hard, when business gets tight, or I hit a wall and need a shift. It became one of my guiding principles.

And if that doesn't work, I go with Plan B: "What would a Jew do?"

Say what you want, but they're some of the smartest business minds in the world. If you're trying to solve a tough problem, that's not a bad mindset to channel.

Back then—this was around 1996—Erwin was making $200,000 a year. For a guy running a Toyota dealership, that was serious money in my eyes. He wasn't flashy about it either. Just handled business.

His words hit me so hard that shortly after, I found myself sitting at the border, just thinking. *What can I do differently? How do I move these cigar boxes more easily and safely?* The problem was, there was no easy way. The borders were airtight—too much drug traffic, too much scrutiny. There weren't any cracks left to slip through.

I'd known Stuart since I was about eight years old. His older brother, Philip, worked at the neighborhood gas station where everyone seemed to know everyone. Stu was always my go-to guy; he knew people from every walk of life. Since he worked at the dealership and Erwin was cool with me, I started using the place like my personal office.

I'd sit in one of the sales cubes, post up with my beeper, a notebook full of customer names and numbers, and just start working the phones. That notebook was like my bible. Inside were the loyal buyers, the maybes, and the ghosts who needed to be reactivated. I'd flip through the pages and focus—almost like meditating—until a name jumped out at me. Then I'd start dialing.

Somehow, it always worked. That book had magic in it.

Even on slow days, when business felt frozen and no one was calling, that quiet space—that cube—gave me room to breathe, focus, and create momentum. It was a privilege to have that setup. I had a desk, a phone, and a chance to bullshit with Stu and the other guys while keeping my hustle alive.

It was in that dealership that I first heard the expression, "The guy closest to the top is closest to the door."

Meaning? When things go sideways, it's usually the manager—not the rookie—who gets fired first. That stuck with me too. Just like Erwin's line.

Because in this life, you learn quickly: staying at the top isn't just about climbing. It's about knowing when to move, when to adapt, and when to find another way.

WISCONSIN LOG CABIN

Once upon a time, I was rolling. I owned the streets, or at least it felt like it. I went looking and found something special: a real log cabin, built from the trees on the same land. Tucked deep in the Wisconsin woods, miles from the nearest town, it was perfect. Private. Quiet. Mine.

It had all the toys: snowmobiles, dirt bikes, a ski boat, and a safe full of guns. It was my little refuge from the world.

But that magic started to fade when the feds began sniffing around.

My sister was living there at the time. She told me federal agents were in town asking questions about me. She even spotted them watching the house from the neighboring property. I was still on the run, and just like that, the place no longer felt secret. No longer safe.

One day, I had to make the trip back up there. I needed to grab something important. I was in a rush. I had just enough time to drive the four and a half hours up and back before an appointment with my federal probation officer the next day. My schedule was packed. The cigars I was waiting on were due to arrive soon, and I needed to be sharp. In my world, if you got sloppy, you got busted.

I made the run, got what I needed, and headed home. Unbeknownst to me, just hours after I left, the cabin caught fire and burned to the ground.

I got back to the city, parked the car, showered, changed clothes, grabbed a quick bite, and headed to my appointment. As I was leaving the building, a UPS truck pulled up. It was my cigars. I had to receive the shipment right then and there—three hundred boxes. No time to bring them upstairs. I signed for the load and stuffed every last box into the trunk of my car.

It was the first and only time I ever did something so risky.

I showed up to my regular probation appointment like nothing was different—except now my trunk was loaded with contraband. Cuban cigars. Hundreds of them. Enough to land me eight years in federal prison if they'd opened that trunk.

The entire time I was there, I was dying inside. I didn't show it, but I was thinking about what might happen. I wanted to turn to water and disappear under the door. I was facing the end of my freedom, standing at the gates of hell, and they might just open and invite me in. Could you imagine the look on their faces if they popped the trunk and saw all those cigars?

To this day, I still think about it. What if they had said, "Let's check your car." If I had their job, I'd do it once in a while, just to see.

And it wasn't just the probation officer waiting that day—it was the ATF. Alcohol. Tobacco. Firearms. The exact agency that would investigate me for Cuban cigars, and I had just dropped myself into their lap.

If they had searched the car? That was it. Game over. And I probably would've caught extra charges for the weapons found in the cabin too. My life, as I knew it, would've been over.

Nobody from probation gave me a heads-up. They just let me walk in. Typical government playbook—keep you in the dark and hit you when you least expect it.

They had a surprise for me. A trap, really.

Inside the office, the ATF agent told me about the fire—how local cops had cracked open a safe, claiming it was an immediate danger. Inside: full-auto machine guns, sawed-off shotguns, military-grade rifles. He said they were impressed with the craftsmanship of the conversions and wanted to know who did the work.

I told him some of the guns belonged to Lopez, a guy who used the cabin and had died a few months earlier. I reminded him, it wasn't my place. My name wasn't on anything. Sure, I'd been there plenty, but I had no idea what was inside that safe. My probation officer sat quietly through the whole thing.

The agent nodded and told me I was free to go. And that was the last I ever heard about it.

The insurance company tried to fight the claim, but with all the local chatter—whispers that maybe it was the feds themselves who started the fire—they eventually backed off and paid out $100,000. We poured every cent straight into the gym.

I was bleeding money, funneling everything I could get my hands on into concrete and steel. The pressure was crushing. There was too much at stake, too much already invested, to ever risk stopping. Halting construction for lack of funds wasn't an option. That would only create new and bigger problems. So I had to keep the cigar money flowing. On top of the construction stress came all the dangers, risks, and uncertainties of the cigar business. Most men would have buckled under that kind of weight. I didn't. That's not bravado; it's just fact.

PACE OF LIFE

It's very uncomfortable to travel thousands of miles only to have customers question the legitimacy of your product, and to be called out on it by people who really don't know what they're talking about.

I had to get better to make my life better. I just had a hard time dealing with the negativity. I was actually traveling to Havana, smuggling the cigars into Mexico, basically traveling across the entire country of Mexico to the USA border, and then smuggling them into the USA, across two border crossings and another 1,500 miles to Chicago.

In the process, the boxes were getting scratched and bruised. The cigars weren't getting damaged, but they weren't being stored correctly for the trip either. I also needed to choose the best quality I could. Brands and sizes were very important too. Most people are followers, so an important part was to have the ones that everyone wanted, which was much easier said than done.

I'll explain the pace of my life at this time.

I'd return from Chicago after a few weeks of waking up early in the morning and driving around a hundred-mile area, stopping at pay phones to call customers and make appointments, making deliveries, collecting money, and all that. Once back in Mexico, I had to make up for the time away. I was always several weeks behind on my work at my business.

I also started to work out every day, even twice a day, to make up for the time I was away. Both in Cuba and Chicago, it's hard to find a chance to work out. I have a wife and two girls to spend time with, and also make up for lost time. All while planning the next Cuba trip. Who would go with me? Would I find the cigars I needed? Could I get the cigars out of Cuba? Would I be able to get them into Mexico without any issues? What border would I take them to? Would I get them across or lose them again?

It was always like a fast train; I was doing so much and thinking so hard.

I also had a full-time business to run, my gym, which was kind of the pride of my life; it was probably the first thing I ever had that was important. I had often daydreamed about owning my own gym when I was in my teens. I would plan it; I was going to make a unique gym. I just knew I could do it right. If I had *my* gym, I would make it different, better than any gym I had seen up to this point in my life.

I was busy from the moment I returned, not only with my business obligations but also with my wife and kids. But I was learning every day, I was in contact with people, and I was always meeting more people and growing my business.

MY FIRST CIGAR CAR

The final day of that Chicago cigar run was sunny and smooth. I'd sold out my inventory, and Oscar—who'd been dragging behind me like dead weight—was off my hands. I didn't leave him stranded either. I introduced him to Wacker, thinking I was doing both of them a favor. They were both in the drug world, and Oscar could be useful to Wacker, or so I believed.

Before leaving, I parked my newly bought Chrysler cigar car outside my mother's suburban apartment, hid the key under the bumper, and flew home to Mexico.

I'd explained the deal to Wacker before leaving: if he wanted to make some easy money, he could drive cars from Chicago to Tucson—no drugs, just cash in the hidden compartments Oscar had told me about. I told Oscar the rules too: no mixing weed with money, no coke, no guns, no pills. Keep it clean. "No powders, pills, or pistols equals no police."

They hit it off instantly. Wacker liked him. I really thought I'd done something good.

Wacker had a car—a Trans Am riddled with bullet holes, still sitting in his family's garage from a shootout at Carson's Ribs years earlier. He didn't have the money to fix it. So when Oscar asked me what I was doing with the Chrysler, I told him I'd be leaving it at my mom's place, just in case of an emergency.

The next morning, I was back in Mexico.

That night, I got the call: "The car's gone." I panicked, checked with management, cops, and towing. Nothing. Then it hit me.

Oscar.

I started calling around and finally got Wacker's little brother, Tommy, on the line. "They left for Tucson," he said. "In your car."

FUCK.

I was furious. They'd stolen my car, and now they were ghosts. I was in the middle of a major construction project, just getting momentum with cigars. And now this.

Weeks later, I got the call: Wacker was in jail in Texas. Bond was high, and Tommy was asking me for help. I didn't give a shit about the bond—I wanted to know where my car was and what the fuck happened.

Turns out they'd driven the Chrysler to Nogales, then tried to pick up a weed load. It fell apart, and Wacker got homesick. Oscar arranged a pickup in Tucson from a guy named Penguin, loaded the car with bales of weed—no compartments, no prep. Just stacked it in the trunk.

Wacker drove—out-of-state plates, registered to a different car entirely.

He got stopped in Texas. Searched. Busted.

Because of his record, they offered him ninety-nine years. He sat inside for nine months before getting bonded out.

I kept pushing cigars, trying not to get pulled back into this bullshit. But Oscar kept calling, asking me to chase Wacker down for the weed money. I couldn't believe it.

"You're trying to collect from a guy facing ninety-nine years?" I asked. "Are you fucking stupid?"

The answer was yes.

Oscar kept bragging about how he was making money, meeting new people, and trying to act like a big shot. But he had no understanding of the code. Of loyalty. Of reality.

He even told me he was going to Wacker's house to take the Trans Am as partial payment. Said Wacker told him to just call first—to make sure the door was open.

But I knew what that meant. Wacker always kept a gun close—usually right in the couch cushions. If Oscar walked into that house, he was going to get shot. No question.

I called Wacker immediately. We hadn't spoken since he got out. I reached him at his dad's house.

He was quiet. Cold. Not his usual self.

I tried to explain—told him Oscar was being stupid, that I was trying to talk him down.

Wacker cut me off. "Scott," he said. "You introduced me to the stupidest person I've ever met in my life. I'm facing ninety-nine years. I'm gonna take it like a man. But don't ever call me again. You're not my friend anymore."

He hung up.

I just sat there, staring at the phone. I was at Grossinger Toyota, using their phone to call my cigar clients, trying to build something. And in that moment, I realized I'd lost Wacker for good.

We'd been friends since we were twelve. He was like a father figure to me. A mentor. A brother.

And now—gone. All because of Oscar.

No good deed goes unpunished.

I tried warning Oscar, over and over. "He'll kill you," I said. "Just stop." But he kept pushing, kept demanding money from a guy who'd gone silent, who'd never cooperated with cops in his life.

Wacker was old-school—a real-deal criminal. Wouldn't even talk to the police. Once, in prison, he got called for a visit. It turned out to be two cops waiting for him. He walked away without a word. "I don't talk to cops." That was Wacker.

And now Oscar was poking the bear, trying to collect a weed debt like this was some kind of office dispute.

It was infuriating. And it was dangerous.

This was the kind of bullshit that kept dragging me back into the past. I was finally making progress, trying to build a clean business. But I couldn't fully escape the kind of people I'd come up with. People like Oscar. People like Wacker.

Oscar destroyed everything he touched. And that included my friendship with Wacker.

I still heard rumors. People talked. Wacker was regressing—hanging out with younger gangbangers, using drugs, dressing like a teenager. I'd heard he wanted me dead.

When a Chicago cop friend called to warn me, it stunned me. But deep down, I wasn't surprised.

He probably heard I was doing well. Building something real. And that's what made it worse.

I gave him my loyalty. My trust. My friendship. And I lost it—all of it—just trying to help a fucking idiot like Oscar.

Chapter Seven

THE COST OF DOING BUSINESS

THE LOGISTIC PROBLEMS WEREN'T THE ONLY PROBLEMS I RAN into. In this business, everyone I met had their hand out, and it was up to me to figure out how to work with them.

Smuggling anything is a dangerous game. You have to worry about everyone and everything. You are fair game to them all; they want to take your product, your money, your freedom, and even your life.

ROBBED AND DISPLACED IN MEXICO CITY

To get to Cuba, I usually had to pass through Mexico City. It had the most frequent flights and was simply the most practical route. Cancun and Guadalajara had flights, too, but either they took longer or weren't consistent. So Mexico City became my stopover.

Back then, Mexico City was the largest city in the world, twenty-four million people. A concrete jungle packed with chaos and danger, like any massive Latin American metropolis. I'd been there many times, especially during my boxing phase, often hitting rough neighborhoods, but usually with locals. That makes all the difference.

One time, my wife and I took a walk near our hotel, passing through a market filled with food vendors. She was wearing a gold ring with diamonds. Right away, my instincts screamed: danger. I caught the eyes of a few young guys clocking the ring. They weren't vendors—just watchers. I told her we needed to go, now. She didn't get it at first. I got angry and pushed her to move. In Mexico City, they'll cut your arm off for gold. Maybe not the guys at the stands, but they'll call someone from the barrio to do it with a gun, knife, or ice pick.

We got out of there. She hid the ring. She eventually understood—nothing happened, but something could have. Mexico City's the kind of place where predators wait in shadows for you to let your guard down.

A few weeks later, I had to go to Cuba again. It was a last-minute trip, so I went alone. I booked a round-trip ticket: Guadalajara to Mexico City to Havana. Like always, I flew into Mexico City the night before. The early morning flights were too risky to catch the same day, and I didn't want to miss it.

I usually stayed at a little dumpy hotel just across from the airport. You'd exit, walk about fifty yards to the overpass, cross it, and there it was. Nothing fancy—about thirty dollars a night. Like most cheap hotels in Mexico, it had the bulletproof glass check-in window, like a currency-exchange booth.

I was wearing denim overalls and a white T-shirt. I had $5,000 hidden in my underwear and a beautiful two-tone Rolex tucked in my chest pocket. I stored my two large suitcases in the airport luggage lockers—this was pre-9/11, when that was still a thing. They gave me a tag and a locker key with a big orange top. I just kept my hygiene bag with me.

I walked across the overpass to the hotel and waited at the window. No one ever came. I went next door—no rooms available. As I stepped outside, a city taxi rolled up—an old-school VW Beetle. These were still popular in Mexico, cheap and compact. No front passenger seat, so you could slide right into the back. The driver had a lever next to him that opened and closed the passenger door.

I had stayed at another hotel not far away a few weeks earlier and told the driver to take me there. I was distracted, planning my Cuba trip in my head. At one point, I noticed he was driving too slowly behind a bus for no reason. I got suspicious but stayed calm. When we arrived, instead of stopping out front, he turned down a dark, deserted side street.

That's when two guys appeared out of nowhere. Dressed in suits with fake police badges, they cornered me just as I started to get out of the Beetle. One foot on the pavement, crouched down, and suddenly I was surrounded.

They said they'd been following me since the airport. Accused me of smuggling drugs. Said we needed to go back and inspect my bags. They shoved me into the back seat between them. Now I had one gun pressed into my ribs and another under my chin.

FUCK. I'm getting killed in Mexico City.

It was a tight space. Only one door. The driver controlled it. These guys had guns already drawn. I stayed calm. I breathed. My animal instinct said "explode," but my survival instinct said "wait."

We drove deeper into the city—dark streets, silent corners. At one point, they spotted a police car and panicked. They shoved my head down and hissed, "Don't move. Don't say a word or I'll kill you right here."

They kept driving. One guy started searching my hygiene bag. Then they frisked me. Hands all over. One reached for my crotch. I flinched. He pressed the gun harder into my jaw and said he'd shoot me and dump me in the street.

They found the five thousand dollars in my underwear. Found the Rolex in my chest pocket. Jackpot.

That was it. I'd been hit. Robbed clean. So I started talking—cracking jokes. Making light of it. Said, "Hey, today you got me. Tomorrow I'll get someone else."

They laughed.

They asked if I was moving weed. I told them cigars. I begged for my hygiene bag and my passport. Explained that without it, I'd need to file a report, stay in town—with it, I'd just vanish. One guy said, "Kill him. He saw our faces." The driver said, "Not in the car." The other guy said, "Let him go."

They opened the door, told me to walk and not look back. I got out. They vanished fast, turning a corner, then another. Gone.

I took off running. I had to get to the airport before they did. They had the key to the luggage locker. I sprinted until I found a small store and burst inside. I told them I'd been robbed. Begged them to point me toward the airport. They said, "Don't run. You'll get robbed again." I told them I had nothing left. One looked at my shoes. "They'll take those too."

I had asked the people from the small store to give me a ride but initially they refused. In the end, he followed me outside and offered to give me a ride back to the airport. Five minutes later, I was back at the airport. I sprinted to the luggage lockers.

When I got there, a guy was already at the window—beaten, bloodied, face swollen. He was American, had been robbed a few hours earlier. Sounded like the same crew. He tried to resist. They beat the shit out of him and took everything.

I was drained. Shaken. No money. Not even enough for a coffee. I called my wife. She had family nearby. Her Uncle Sergio—an architect and good guy—came and picked me up. Gave me food, a place to crash, and a few pesos. I'd missed my flight. I'd have to go back to Guadalajara, regroup, and try again later.

But I had a fire in my gut. I was gonna hunt those bastards down.

The next night, I went back to the airport, watching for familiar faces. But to my surprise, everyone looked like them. Every guy—five feet tall, dark skinned, short hair. I couldn't tell them apart. I stared at every face, convinced I'd know them. But the truth hit me hard.

There was no way to find them. Even if one walked up and introduced himself, I wouldn't know for sure.

So what did I do?

I licked my wounds and moved forward. My pride was bruised. I was angry. But it was my fault—I let my guard down.

I've said it before: Latin America isn't the good ol' USA. You talk too much, show off, flash a watch or a wad of cash—you're asking for it. You have to move in silence. No ego. No boasting.

THE BOSS OF MEXICO CITY

My Cuban friend Elier and I were both having trouble getting our cigars into Mexico; it was getting harder and harder. More people were doing it, and it was getting messy. There were people from all over the world now traveling to Cuba to get cigars and smuggle them back to their own countries.

Since Mexico was close and there were several direct flights, Mexico got overloaded with cigar smugglers. Mexico City, Cancun, and Guadalajara all had direct flights coming in from Cuba. It was then possible to transfer anywhere in the world. In the beginning, it was different; now it was getting messy. The Mexican authorities were always looking to make a buck, so they were now hunting for cigars. This meant they could take your bags away (and later steal them and sell them) or threaten to take them away and make you pay. Either way, it was getting messy.

Elier and I decided to hook up in Mexico City to see if we could work out something. I had my wife and two of my employees in Cuba on a buying trip, and I had to get something arranged for their arrival at the airport.

Elier had now arrived in Mexico City, so I went to the airport to pick him up. We immediately started walking around the airport randomly talking to agents, airport employees, etc. The first day didn't produce anything. We had spent about five hours inside the airport and hadn't come up with anything useful. We left the airport and went to get a hotel room.

The next day, I went to his room to get our day started, and I was standing there waiting for him to finish up so we could go back to the airport and get a fresh start on our mission. All of a sudden, I started to feel dizzy. This always happens to me before an earthquake! Then the whole building started to move.

Elier shouted, "It's moving! It's shaking! Earthquake!"

We took off like wild animals down the three flights of stairs and out into the middle of the street. There were already thousands of people in the street. People in Mexico City are very scared of earthquakes; they had a terrible one in 1984, and thousands of people died. It was a surreal feeling to live through this. It makes you paranoid for the next few days, if not weeks or months.

Then the two of us were back at the airport, on a mission. We had spoken to many people and probably made ourselves known. We had walked the airport from one side to the other more times than I could count, and we were probably now being watched. We eventually decided to try to get into the customs area, but it was guarded, and there was no entrance, only an exit. This was international arrivals, and when flights came in from certain places, they would be heavily scrutinized, so we knew the bosses and the guys with the final word would be there sometimes, at least. Again, we tried to get in, we asked a few people questions; we had probably been there for two hours when three agents approached us.

They were all wearing suits and had their badges and credentials around their necks. We already knew that the PGR had a black ID badge. They came out just to see us because the word was getting around that we had been poking around for the last few days.

The only guy to speak asked us, "What the fuck do you want?" He was tense and aggressive; he didn't know who we were or what we wanted. We tried to lift the tension by smiling and shaking hands. He relaxed a little. "Okay, white boy (*weto*), what do you want? What drugs do you want to pass through?"

I explained that it was a suitcase of cigars. He smiled and said, "Don't bullshit me. You can pass anything you want, but you have to pay!"

I insisted, "It's Cuban cigars, only cigars." He looked back at one of the other guys, and they made eye contact, and the other guy kind of nodded and affirmed that it was something they were seeing more often.

He now smiled and said, "Sure, it's four hundred dollars a suitcase." He gave me his number and told me to call him. I told him I had someone coming in soon and had to get a guarantee. He smiled and said, "I'm the comandante of the whole airport."

Finally, I had the contact I needed: Armando, the boss of the Mexico City airport.

I was elated; it felt like I was floating on the clouds. I had a few people in Havana just waiting for me to let them know I had everything arranged for their arrival at the Mexico City airport.

I called Armando and we agreed to meet at a restaurant in the airport at 1:00 p.m., and my people arrived at 2:00 p.m. I met him at a Wings café; it's a diner-type restaurant, similar to a Denny's. We sat down, ordered food, and began to talk. He turned out to be friendly and likable. He was about five feet five, had dark skin, and wore dark suits.

He again asked me what I was bringing. He told me, "I don't care what your product is, but if you lie to me, I'll FUCK you." He asked again if it was drugs, and I assured him it was cigars. He told me he had people bringing everything. He had someone who brought live animals from Africa: lions, tigers, snakes, monkeys, everything.

My people were landing now with about six large suitcases. They would all be registered all the way to GDL with a bright orange tag for everyone to see. We finished up our meal and headed to the arrivals. He now had two guys waiting outside the restaurant. We all started walking toward the arrivals, and we were late. People were already coming out with Havana bag tags.

He walked through the exit doors as if he owned the place. We were now inside the baggage claim area. I saw my people; they were all being detained by customs agents. They looked frustrated and scared. They were animated and deep into their explanations.

I told Armando that those were my people and suitcases. He calmly walked over to where they were, flashed his badge, and took over. He even helped carry the heavy bags, and then we all walked out the front door. We kept walking until we were about thirty yards away from the arrivals exit. We stopped, and he motioned to his guys; they proceeded to open a few bags, they saw cigar boxes everywhere, and they gave him a look to affirm.

He and I walked a few feet away and took cover behind a large round post. I had the cash counted, separated, and ready for him in my pocket. I gave him the cash without even attempting to be discreet. He couldn't care less. He gave me a paper with his home phone number, and we each went our own way.

I went back to my group, who were still kind of in shock. First, they were being questioned and detained, and then out of nowhere, I came through the exit doors with three guys who could overrule the cops who had them. They were escorted out of there and set free with all of the suitcases. Again, another good moment.

HABANOS INVOICE

Since I had been waiting in Mexico City, I had some free time while in the city, so I decided to check out a few cigar shops. I was always hungry to learn more—not just about selling cigars, but understanding them: the culture, the packaging, the details. It all mattered.

I made my way to the official Habanos cigar store. It wasn't huge, but it had a decent variety. I loved just being around cigars—the smell, the look of the boxes, the artistry of the labels. To me, they were beautiful.

And then it hit me.

As I browsed, I noticed something: every single box of Cuban cigars had an import sticker—a clean, official label with all the import information. Every box. Like a lightbulb going off in my head, I saw it: this could be my solution.

This was the cover I needed.

A way to move cigars without drawing heat from the cops. Something to show if I ever got stopped. It was brilliant—one of those rare, perfect little moments that change the game.

I bought a box on the spot, paid full retail, didn't care. It was worth it. And not just the cigars. I was asked to pay the tax too. I wanted the official invoice. I needed that receipt in my hands. Proof. Something real. Something clean.

I walked out of that store with the biggest grin on my face. That box with its sticker and receipt wasn't just a box of cigars anymore.

It was a blueprint. A new layer to the hustle.

THE INVOICE SYSTEM

Back home in Guadalajara, I reached out to my friend William, my go-to printer. He'd done a lot of work for my businesses over the years. Advertising, flyers, business cards—all kinds of printing. He was also a member of my gym. Bilingual. His dad was American, but William was 100 percent Mexican in the way he lived and operated.

I went to his office and showed him the import sticker and the official invoice I'd brought back from the Habanos store. The invoice had those legit-looking red serial numbers—the kind that start at 0001 and go up. I had him begin mine somewhere in the one thousands. I didn't want to raise any red flags by using low numbers that looked like I'd just started printing them yesterday.

The invoices also had a legal notice printed on them. They looked real because they were real—or at least close enough to pass. It was technically illegal to print documents like that, but William made it happen.

And now, I had a weapon.

These weren't just pieces of paper. They were tools. Tools I could use to shut down any cop or checkpoint. If I got stopped, I had everything the law required: the import sticker on the box, and the official-looking invoice in my hand.

And it worked.

Like magic.

Cops would pull me over, ask questions, start probing, and then I'd show them the paperwork. And just like that, the conversation was over. They backed off. I was no longer just some guy with a trunk full of Cuban cigars. Now I looked legit. Small details like this made all the difference in the world. They may seem small, but they were game changers.

Sometimes the best way to beat the system is to learn how to fake being inside it.

The beginning. Oscar and me in Laredo, crossing my first load of cigars into Texas and praying the plan worked.

My first major cigar purchase—bought from Arturo Brigante, my first Cuban supplier in Mexico. This was the load I later smuggled with Oscar.

Humidifiers that I made and sold to my clients. The one on the right is a humidifier that I still keep in my office.

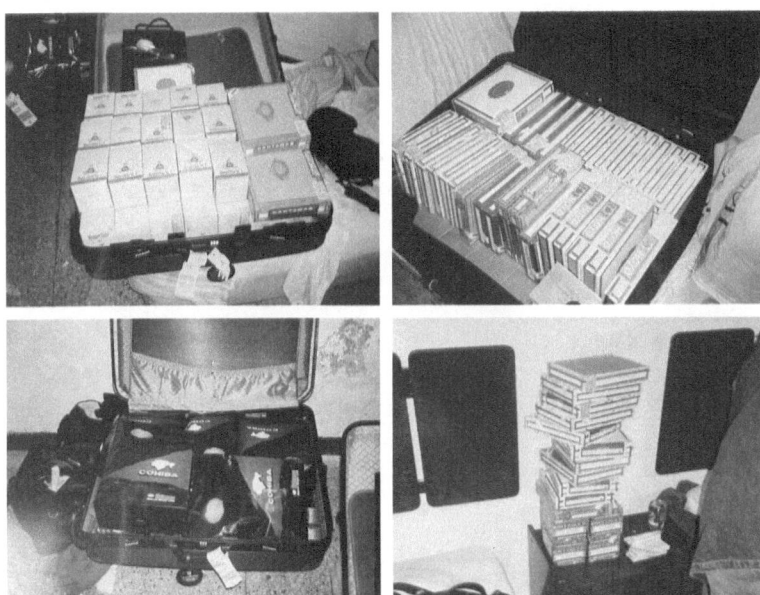

Packing the cigars.

THE COST OF DOING BUSINESS · 117

I turned a closet into a walk-in humidor with nothing more than a hydrometer and a water humidifier. It kept thousands of cigars fresh as they moved across two countries.

Havana cigar factory, 1990s.

Some of the original cards from factories and official stores.

(25 PUROS)

PRODUCTO CUBANO ENVASADO
DE ORIGEN
ELABORADO Y EXPORTADO POR
CORPORACION HABANOS,S.A.
MERCADERES No.21
HABANA,CUBA.
IMPORTADO Y DISTRIBUIDO POR:
IMPORTADORA Y EXPORTADORA DE
@#!*#%&#$*!%& S.A. DE C.V.
%&@#!*##$*!%&%&@#!*##$*!%&
@#!*##$*!%&%&%&@#!*##
!%&%&@#!#
R.F.C. EJM 951103 H34
DEJAR DE FUMAR
REDUCE IMPORTANTES
RIESGOS EN LA SALUD.

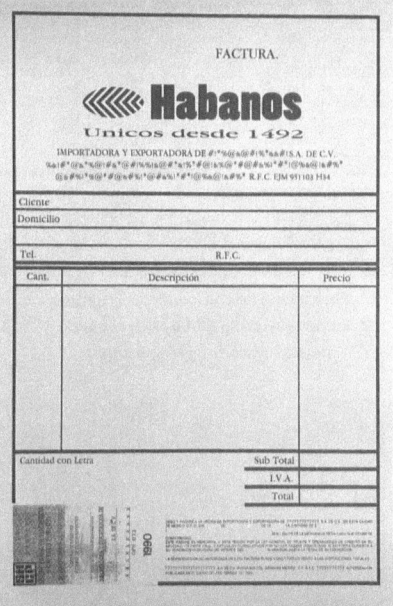

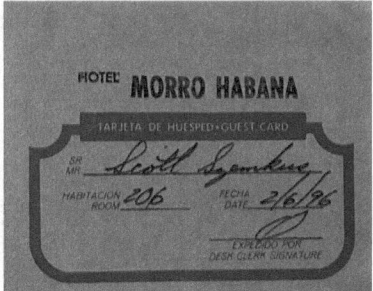

Fake import stickers and Habanos invoices I created to make my cigars look official in Mexico—simple tricks that saved me more times than I can count.

Guest cards from the Havana hotels and nightclubs that became part of my life during those years.

Me and my friend Eduardo Trujillo, who traveled to Cuba with me and helped me smuggle the cigars.

Me and my driver Jaime. While we were in Cuba, we didn't drive, we always had a driver. So he was by my side most of the time.

Me and Ernesto López, general director of Partagás.

Me and Enrique Mons from La Casa del Habano on 5th Avenida. On the paper it says, "Hi Mark." This is because Enrique told me he was also friends with Marc Hauser.

My friend Toño López, having a good time in Cuba.

Photo of my friend Arturo Brigante, when I made my first purchase of Cuban cigars from him.

My first driver, Luigi. He always drove luxury cars in Cuba.

Me with Abel Exposito, then manager of the Partagás factory store.

Me and Andrea with special-order, hand-rolled torpedoes—no mold, all skill.

THE COST OF DOING BUSINESS · 123

Girls of Cuba.

Front-page news in Nogales, Arizona: the night nearly 5,000 of my cigars were seized in the mountains.

THE COST OF DOING BUSINESS · 125

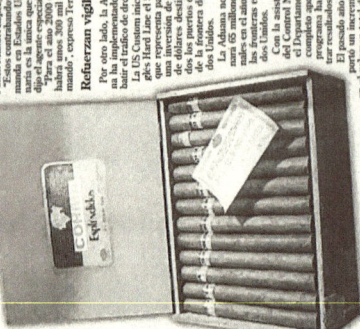

Nogales, Mexico put it on the front page too—same seizure, almost 5,000 of my cigars gone that night.

The headline even claimed cigar smuggling was more profitable than drug trafficking.

Cuban newspaper article about the illegal smuggling of street and bad-quality cigars.

It was rumored that Fidel Castro had his own exclusive cigar brand, Trinidad, reserved for gifts for kings and dignitaries. Here is the book I found with Fidel's signature, which became one of the tools I used to create the brand.

Some of the stamps I used in my work, including the one taken from Fidel's book-cover signature, which I later pressed into my cigar boxes.

Muscular Development magazine (August 2003) pp. 246–247. Article by John Romano about our travel to Cuba.

DIGS WERE A DONE DEAL

It seems that many years ago, long since the statute of limitations ran out, Scott made 60 or 70 trips to Havana smuggling the finest Cuban cigars out of the country, through Mexico, and selling them in Chicago.

SEX-PECTATIONS

For several days leading up to the trip, Scott recounted story after story of the exploits he and his cigar mules experienced at the hands of ultra-willing Cuban babes.

"Welcome to Cuba," Scott said. "After the revolution, Castro took over the real estate. Many of the people who lived in these places fled the country after Batiste was overthrown and Castro took the houses and the land. They belong to the state now, as does everything else. Other homes were second or third homes of prominent Cubans. Castro said, 'Okay, you get one house, which one is it going to be?' He took the others. The ones that are all fixed up are foreign embassies. They rent them from the government."

The next couple of days pretty much ran into each other. We slept late, trained hard and partied even harder. We walked through downtown and Old Havana smoking fine Cuban cigars, and went to La Bogedita del Medio, the famous bar where Ernest Hemmingway used to hang out.

Excerpts of the article I'm mentioned in, "Cuba, The Next Bodybuilding Oasis?" by John Romano.

The foundation of my dreams: my gym, under construction.

A current photo of me and my friends
Eduardo Trujillo and Arturo Brigante.

A current photo of me and my friends
Toño López and Eduardo Trujillo.

A current photo of me and my friend Luis Arrollo.

Me with football players Shaun Gayle and Richard Dent.

Here's a photo with my friend Marc Hauser, a famous photographer who worked with many celebrities, including Michael Jordan.

THE COST OF DOING BUSINESS · 133

Signed Michael Jordan jersey that hangs in
my office—a gift I've kept for years.

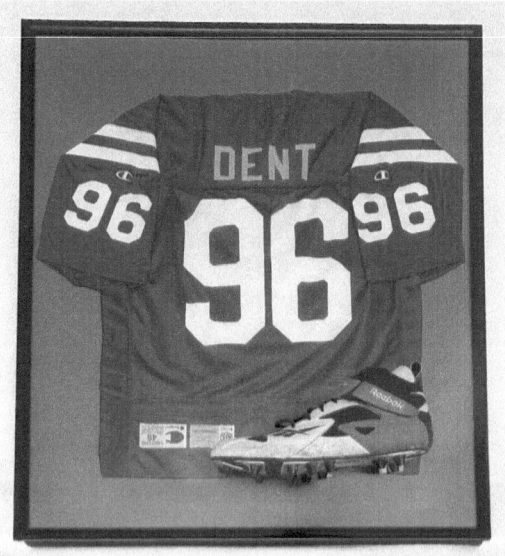

Richard Dent's game-used cleat from his Chicago Bears days
and his signed Colts jersey—both displayed in my office.

With Michael Jordan at his home. I'm in my socks because we were in his kitchen, not a photo op.

With my friend Howard Frum—the "Rolex King of Chicago." Without Howard, none of this would have been possible.

Chapter Eight

BUSTED

MY WIFE AND I WENT OUT WITH RAUL (THE CUSTOMS AGENT) and his wife; he was a little different from most people. He insisted that we stay at his brother's house, but we already had a room paid for at the hotel. But he insisted. Since I was trying to stay in his good graces, I convinced my wife we could do it. The house was a single-story home in the Guanabacoa neighborhood, well-known for a lot of witchcraft. The house was bare; I'm sure it hadn't been painted in thirty years, no air conditioning, no hot water, an old spring bed, and no screens on the windows. The bathroom was on the other side of the backyard.

There were no curtains on the windows, and at some point in the night, we both woke to a Black man staring at us through the window. The mosquitoes were beyond unbearable, but it was the roosters crowing at sunup that finally made me throw in the towel. For the next few days, we slept at our hotel and showed up at this house in the morning to drink coffee with Raul and his wife.

They were very nice people, small people in a very small life, and just trying to make it. Raul's brother was a doctor, a highly qualified doctor. He, like many other doctors, had a several-square-block area where he was assigned, and the people in this area were his patients. He lived with the hope that one day he could benefit from all his years of studying. He made only eight dollars per month.

When it was time to leave, I told Raul I had fourteen bags. I met him the night before we left and gave him $1,200.

The next day, I stopped at Capi's on the way to the airport to pick up more bags. I had a minivan taxi loaded to the gills with cigars. Capi had made some pretty good money with me so far and was packing for a planned trip. He helped me down the three flights of stairs with the bags and then helped me pack them into the van. Off to the airport we went. We arrived as scheduled and unloaded all the suitcases curbside.

As I'm looking around for a luggage cart, I'm approached by a young guy who gets real close and tries to whisper in my ear. I don't really hear him, because he's apparently trying to be discreet. I did hear "Raul" and "only two suitcases." I'm lost. What did he say? What was going on? What I understood or what I thought he had said was that Raul said to only come with two suitcases. I had the van turn around and drove all the way back to Capi's apartment. There, we unloaded all but four bags, two each. If the driver of the van wasn't suspicious before, he was now for sure, and all the commotion probably gave it away.

We went back to the airport, and it was now almost dark, but we still had time to make the flight if everything went smoothly. There wasn't much of a line at the Mexicana Airlines counter. We walked directly up to the counter, and from behind me, I was touched on the back. I turned to see Raul. I told him everything was cool, and we only had two suitcases each. He was cold and removed; he didn't really look at me, but said, "No, it's not good. Just keep your mouth shut and follow me."

There were now several agents surrounding us. They led us out the front door of the airport and into the arrivals part on the other side of the airport. I was calm but wary. WTF was happening? My suitcases were out on a table in the customs area, and they were all emptied, about 125 boxes out there for everyone to see. It looked like a mountain. They had experts studying them; they had accountants; it was very formal. After a few hours, it was apparent we weren't making our flight.

The whole ordeal took about four hours. Raul finally said our passports would be held until further notice. I was given a number to call each day. That was it. We were being held on the island until they figured out what to do with us. We went back to Capi's, where he was nervously waiting for us. He had to go, but he was gracious enough to let us stay in his apartment. He knew this was a mess and that it could blow up in our faces.

Capi went on his trip and left us in his apartment. It was a strange feeling. We were basically being detained but free to wait around.

I got in contact with Raul, and we met at a remote area near his house. He didn't have an easy way to come see me. He apologized for what had happened and said they had brought in a special team at the last moment. He was removed from his post and sent to the other side. He told me that he had told the young guy to give me a letter, the guy had put it into my pocket, and I had never seen it. He told me I would be released soon and that I would be given a court date. The person who would hear my case was his friend and would help me through it.

He returned my $1,200 and again apologized. He was scared—very scared. This wasn't a game for him; this was his life. He could get into serious trouble because of something like this.

I called the number I was given each day as instructed, and I was finally told I would be leaving the next day on the same evening flight. I was instructed to come early and go to their office.

I still had at least ten suitcases plus loose boxes here at Capi's apartment, and I had to figure out how to get them out of here and back to my humidor. The next day, we went to the airport as instructed. It had been four days since we were detained. We reported to their office and had to go through some paperwork. They returned our passports and tickets to travel. To my surprise, they had two of our suitcases there with about fifteen boxes per case. They allowed us to have what an appropriate amount might be. I was given a court date a month away. We were then let out and on our own.

Once we got through the checkpoint and into the waiting area, I met a drunk American guy, Larry. He was in a great mood, and he started bragging to me about who he was and what he did, and who he knew. He was there for cigars too. He had receipts for expensive boxes, special editions, and so on. He was on his way to Mexico City, where he had a contact to get his cigars into Mexico, and from there he would transfer to a flight for Juárez/El Paso, Texas.

As he was boasting, a light bulb went off in my head. You see, he bought only factory cigars, no street cigars, no bullshit. He mentioned a few details and dropped a few names that stuck in my head, especially in light of what had just happened. That's when I got interested in buying factory cigars. The few times I had been in there to inquire before, it didn't go well. They were not friendly and claimed to have none. The few boxes I saw were already sold, they would say. But this guy Larry was getting what he wanted, and I can tell you he wasn't anything special. Larry was a trust-fund kid. His father left him a trust that gave him $10,000 a month. All he needed to do was get from one month to the next, and his game started all over again.

Like many times in my life, someone or something was put in my path to wake me up or help me. I truly believe Larry was one of those people. This set a whole new trajectory for me. Larry and I spoke during most of the flight back to Mexico City. We exchanged numbers and each went on our way.

Cigars were getting more popular, and the growth was fast and intense. With this came more cigar tourism and more problems. So many people were coming to Cuba to get cigars out, and their first choice was always street cigars, cheap and accessible. Yes, you can fool yourself, but street cigars are not the same as factory cigars, and they definitely were not available on a steady basis. One hundred percent of all the issues I had had up until now were because I had street cigars and also because of my lack of cigar knowledge and experience.

RETURN TO HAVANA

Three weeks had passed since my incident at the Havana airport. Antonio and Eduardo had gone back and gotten some of the other suitcases with no problem, but I still had a lot of suitcases left. So I got a bunch of guys together by advertising "Free trip to Cuba" in my gym. A guy named Luis signed up, and I was ready to go back.

I decided to fly in alone and on a completely separate reservation from the rest of my guys. I planned to fly in one day before them.

I landed at the José Martí International Airport, Havana, Terminal 2, and I was outside pretty fast. I had already agreed to meet Raul at a gas station about a mile away. My appointment was at Terminal 1 airport, which was about two miles away. You could see it from Terminal 2, but it wasn't connected. I took a taxi there and spoke to him about what to expect. He told me that the woman in charge was the same one he had told me about, and she would help me. I got to the airport a few minutes before my scheduled appointment. It was a very small airport and very outdated, or plainly stuck in 1950. I was led to an office around the corner from the entrance. It had just a few desks and a chair. I took a seat and waited. No one on this island is ever in a hurry to get anything done, so I waited and waited.

Finally, she came in, and we went over my receipts that she already had. They had an older man come in to inspect both the receipts and some of the boxes. He never said anything, made no comments, nor had any facial expressions. He was obviously an expert on cigars and could identify a fake very easily. Hell, I could now almost identify a fake box, and he had probably been doing this his whole life. I didn't want to be there, but I felt I had to be there. I could have just blown it off like they probably thought I would, but then I might have this hanging over me like a rain cloud that could pop at any time.

I don't know what I was thinking, even trying to get them back, since I still didn't know much about them myself. I thought maybe I could slip through the cracks; also, I didn't want to lose my contact with Raul. He had told me since the beginning, "only factory cigars," but of course, I lied, and they were all street cigars. I probably could have gotten in a lot of trouble trying to get them back, and this woman probably helped me avert that.

I had only been selling cigars for about six months then, and it looked promising; I didn't want to ruin everything. I still had high hopes for MY cigar-selling future.

Nothing happened, nothing at all…I didn't get my cigars back, and they didn't tell me anything. She told me they would look further into the matter, and I should stay in contact. That was it. I walked out the front door and went to find a place to stay.

Let's get one thing straight right now—a cigar is a fuckin' cigar. It's a bunch of leaves wrapped just right so it burns correctly, that's it. If those leaves happen to grow in Cuba, then you get a Cuban cigar. If a person is a skilled cigar roller, they can make a cigar the same whether they're working at home or sweating away in the factory, using stolen leaves or government-owned. The tools used to roll a cigar are simple, even primitive, and easy to get.

Finding exactly what I wanted in Havana wasn't always simple. Certain brands and sizes were often scarce. On the streets, 100 percent of cigars were either stolen or made from stolen products. It wasn't like the guys could just put in an order for me. The average Cuban didn't give a damn about cigars; they cared about eating. They sold whatever brand they happened to have in their possession. I had at least fifty different sources I could buy from, and new ones offering me deals every day, but I needed quality. That was the hard part. I became a Cuban cigar connoisseur. As I evolved, so did the cigar market. I needed the best, and on the streets, that wasn't easy. You could find them, sure, but only with persistence and a sharp eye. Some brands were almost impossible to get, both on the street and from the factories.

What most guys don't want to hear is that they've bought and smoked street cigars, and that street cigars and factory cigars are often the same fuckin' thing. Sorry to burst your bubble, but if you've smoked Cuban cigars, the odds are close to 100 percent that you've smoked "street cigars."

For whatever reason, it bothered me to sell "street cigars" to my customers. It shouldn't have, but it did. I've always had a certain kind of honor. I'd rather stick a gun in someone's face to rob them than con them. I didn't like to lie and scam to make my money. If the cigars are put together right (it's not brain surgery), there's not a smoker in the world who could tell the difference—not one. But the profits were so much higher than factory cigars, and the inventory was so much better. That's the allure for guys like me from all over the world.

That's why so many guys smuggled and sold street cigars—the fuckin' profit was off the charts. Imagine pulling a box off the streets of Havana for twenty bucks and flipping it for a thousand in the States. That kind of margin doesn't just make you money—it gets in your blood. The allure wasn't just the cash. It was the chase, the hustle, and the feeling of beating the system. The rush was so strong, it made every risk feel worth it.

SEX AND POVERTY

I went to the airport with Luigi to pick up the guys, Antonio, Eduardo, Luis A, and Luis, the guy who answered the ad "Free Trip To Cuba." They were scheduled for four days in Cuba. We all packed ourselves into the little car and drove toward the city, a bunch of suitcases loaded on the roof and the trunk open with bags everywhere. We went directly to the small Paladar that we had eaten at before: fresh grilled fish, rice, and beans…simple and healthy.

This was the first time we had all been together; the new guy, Luis, was very uncomfortable, and I could just see it in his face. He was not like these animals. He was gay. The guy was suffering, but genuine. These guys are as close to cavemen as can be, and the way they speak and what they speak about, just not who, he was ready to run the other way. This guy was refined; he had taste and some class. These guys were barbaric. He wanted out of that restaurant so bad I could feel his need and urgency. I had initially told them about the new apartment, and he was also invited, but he made up a quick excuse and was gone. "I got a phone number of a friend," he told me, and that I could always get hold of him via this number. He didn't waste any time. He didn't want a ride; he just wanted to be gone. The guy had a good job at the Thai Embassy and was just an innocent person who answered a simple ad for a free trip.

The rest of us piled back into the car and drove to our new apartment. We unloaded and met the hosts. They were a twenty-eight-ish married couple with some other family members hanging around. They immediately asked us if we had any Carmelo's candy or chocolate. Everyone asked for this, even the cops and immigration police at the airport. A guy could literally get laid for a chocolate bar, no lie; it's the truth.

I really didn't need to be looking for more cigars, but it was just in my nature, even though I had about eight suitcases, two for each guy. I was still interested to check out the products and at least see what was available. You never really know what you may find.

If I got all the stuff I had at Capi's, I would feel relieved. I remember how much I had thought about what had happened. I kept thinking of Larry. This guy had it much better; he didn't even worry about the airport. Hell, they had his stuff delivered to him there or escorted. Here I was doing it the hard way, just like the rest of my life, doing it the hard way.

The first one to bring a girl back was Louie. He went down to the beach and met her walking. They hung out at the beach for a few, took some sun, and came back to the apartment to fuck. She was a very pretty girl, nineteen-ish, curly, bushy black hair, and she was friendly and nice. She was gone as fast as she had appeared. Antonio and Eduardo were very active; those two had a lot more experience in Havana and felt like kings while there.

The owner of the apartment introduced me to his fifteen-year-old daughter; he pushed her very hard on me. I finally told him he didn't need to do that with me. I gave him a tip at the end of the stay. I also told him she was too young, so he brought his niece, who was like eighteen.

This may sound very immoral and perverted to most of you, but you're not Cuban. To them, this was not only normal, but it could be the beginning of lifesaving changes to their lives. Men often go crazy for women, and they get generous. This means a better life for the whole family. Sex, what value does that have? The women sold or rented their bodies, but their hearts and souls belonged to their families.

Havana was overloaded with girls from all over the island. They came just for this reason, to find and meet foreigners. It was common to see exceptionally beautiful girls walking down the street with a small backpack, and all these girls were available. They weren't selling it; they didn't have a flat fee. It was just the beginning of whatever. Worst case, they would get a meal or two; best case, a change of lifestyle. I have been offered girls more times than I can count: daughters, cousins, neighbors, wives, sisters, nieces. It was never meant to be offensive. They were sincerely offering, maybe the only thing they had to offer, to just get some money to buy something they needed, even just food.

On this very day, everyone was hungover. They got up late, and we had to go pick up Tono and Eddy from some other place. I was way past starving and needed food badly. Again, the four of us packed into Luigi's little Russian shit box of a car. We were driving down the street, and someone commented about gays.

Luigi then tells us a story about a Spaniard who hires him as a driver, part of which boasts that he has an international clientele. He goes on to describe how the Spaniard asked him if he could help him get young boys, blonds with blue eyes, preferably, thirteen-year-olds with parental consent. We were mostly just daydreaming and not paying too much attention as we made our way to food. He then says he tells the Spaniard he might be able to help, but would need to know how much he's offering to pay. The Spaniard says 1,500 euros. Luigi now gets animated and yells, "How about me?"

Now the whole car is laughing. Boy Luigi, you're really funny, hahaha, what a good joke. Luigi gives a very serious look and says, "No joke. For $1,500, all of you can do whatever you want to me."

This is a twenty-five-year-old heterosexual, married with a baby, willing to get fucked in his ass by five guys for some money. That's really sad. Americans have no idea how good a life they really have.

We were all quiet for a long moment. I'm sure everyone thought about the seriousness of what he had just said. Wow. We didn't joke about it with him ever again. This was a true-life tragedy.

YA VALIO MADRE TODO

We were all set for the next day. We all needed to arrive at the airport at the same time, three hours before flight time. The flight was scheduled for 5:00 p.m., which meant we needed to be there at 2:00 p.m. at the latest.

I was told not to be late, and I told my guys, "You must be on time!"

This is so difficult when dealing with young men, and now add to that they are Mexicans, always late, and never take anything too seriously. I called the friend of the guy, Luis, and told him how important it was to be on time. I called several times to make sure. I even called a few hours before we needed to be there. I told my guys as many times as I could because this time I wouldn't be with them. I was on a different reservation and wanted to remain distant from them. Louie and I were the only ones who spoke English and Spanish; the rest spoke only Spanish.

As usual, they all went out the night before we left; they all stayed out the whole night and defiled themselves. No one but me was there on time. I was there and that was it. I was in and out, trying to figure out how to make a call and how to track them down.

They finally started showing up about an hour before the flight. I had been checked in since I got there. I didn't even want to give any signs that we knew each other. I saw Luigi outside, and I went to talk to him.

"What the fuck?" I asked him. "You fucking knew better. It's too late. They can't check in now."

He went in to try to talk to them, but they all just brushed him off as a fool.

I had to go through security, and Louie went with me. We were on the outside, and there was absolutely no way to see on the other side past immigration. We were just stuck waiting. Time was barely moving. It felt for a moment like time had frozen. The airline was already boarding, and they were herding us toward the bus that would transport us to the plane.

Out of the side of security came a customs agent carrying two of the bags. At the same time, I heard Antonio yell, "Scott! *Ya valio Madre todo* (It's all fucked)."

At that moment, Eduardo came through the immigration gates, he came through security, and came straight to me, right in my face, and he said, "They want invoices." I had the invoices and tried to give them to him, but the airline people were literally pulling, dragging, and pushing me out of there.

I was torn. I couldn't leave them behind. It was all mine, and they really had nothing to do with it. I stopped hard. I told them I had the invoices and I needed to help. The Cuban woman said, "You need to get out of here. There's nothing you can do to help them except get on that plane and get away."

I didn't say a word. I stepped back onto the bus, and at that moment, Eduardo rushed onto the bus. He looked like he wanted to cry. "Give me the invoices!"

I gave him the invoices, and he slowly backed out of the bus.

Before long, all the bags could be seen at the security checkpoint. Too many. At that moment, it looked like too much. Like a scene from a movie, it was going from close to far vision, like in a tunnel. My world was unraveling right in front of me, and there was nothing I could do.

The plane we were boarding was the type that had the stairs directly up the rear end. It was a long, narrow staircase right into the plane. I just kept stalling. I was really suffering, but they kept pushing me.

Again, they told me, "You don't know how lucky you are to be leaving. Don't be stupid."

I had told Louie, "Hey, go back there with them."

He said, "Fuck you, there's no way I'm going back there."

As the plane was taxiing, we could see commotion back at the small airport. We then saw them getting into cars and Jeeps. They were coming for us on the plane. Luis and I watched as we took off by the grace of God. We were on our way back to Mexico City, just the two of us and no cigars.

I just lost four hundred boxes of cigars and a lot of suitcases. Each suitcase was a loss of a lot of money too. Some were a few hundred each.

In my head, I was going over and over what happened. I kept telling myself that it couldn't be so bad; it was only cigars.

I just kept thinking...why? Was I being watched? Was it because they showed up late? Did someone turn me in?

I got home and sat down with my wife. She couldn't feel my pain, and she definitely didn't give a shit about any of the guys I left behind. I did. I was suffering. I decided to go talk to my Cuban friend Elier. I drove to his house; he was home. I told him the story, and he, too, was surprised. He had heard and lived many stories as a Cuban, but it wasn't common for tourists to be overly scrutinized by the authorities.

He and I went over everything, all the details, trying to pinpoint something, but we really couldn't. He said he would make some calls to people in Cuba. He showed me his new phone, a "flip" phone, and let me use it.

I started calling everyone and anyone I had ever met in Cuba or was involved with in Cuba. I called the airport, the airlines, the travel agent, the restaurant in the airport, Raul and Diego (the two customs agents), everyone. This is the way to get shit done. You must be persistent and relentless. It helps if you're also a likable person and can elegantly kiss some ass too.

I got some information from the airline employees. They said that all three of my guys were put into handcuffs and taken away by the police. They were also able to confirm that their ticket status was "pending." This was more than I could get from anywhere else. I was trying to find Capi and his son, Luigi, but they had gone into hiding, probably fearing for their lives.

EVERYONE SINGS

I was going over and over what Raul had told me, that you don't want to go to the secret police station *Todos Cantan* ("Everyone Sings"). Now it was a reality.

Time went by so slowly, it was agonizing. I was really concerned for the guys. This was in my front pocket. But in the back pocket was the loss of all of my cigars, bags, money, and more, but also the future of my cigar business. It would be so much more complicated if I had to depend on other people bringing me the cigars, and much more expensive too.

The pressure was building. I was getting calls from Antonio and Eddy's families. At first, my wife redirected the calls, and it worked, but as the days passed, they started to become aggressive.

Antonio's father yelled at my wife, "Where the fuck is my son?"

I was really running at full speed all day. Thanks to the special cell phone I had, at least I could call everywhere all the time without it costing my left arm.

Capi looked at me one day while I was in the middle of moving and shaking, making calls, and meeting people. He said, "Scott, it's amazing. I've lived in Cuba my whole life, and you know more people than me. I did too. I knew people everywhere and had to.

I used the phone so much that I had to buy a special battery box to keep it charged, as I burned up the phone all day long. We were on day three or four, I was out to eat at Sirloin Stockade buffet, and there was Antonio's father and brother. Now it was really going to be a big deal! I really felt like a piece of shit. I'm back home, eating all you can eat, and these guys are probably being tortured twenty-four hours a day.

There was nothing I could do, either, except wait. I still called everyone and would only get small bits and comments, mostly people's opinions.

After a long and grueling seven days, I finally got the call I'd been waiting for. They were out, but not free. Their passports hadn't been returned, and they were ordered to remain in the country until further notice. It's exactly what they had done to me when I was detained.

Are they investigating you? Are they making you stay longer just to make you suffer? Or is it about money? Are they forcing you to spend more before they let you leave? Whatever the reason, it's torture. Your imagination runs wild, feeding you the worst scenarios. You're stranded on an island, trapped under antiquated laws, while facing hard justice and severe consequences.

Antonio called me. At the end of the day, he wasn't that affected. They were alive and free on the Island of Cuba. They spoke Spanish and had a zest for life. Most Mexicans know how to enjoy life. They just live richer, more indulgent lives, or are just hooked on immediate gratification. They told me Capi had hooked them up with a place to stay, and he gave them my $1,200 that was supposed to guarantee letting my cigars past without an issue. So I also know the agent didn't get in trouble. It was most likely that because they didn't show up on time as requested, three hours before flight time.

Many moving parts needed to be arranged by the agent in the back. First, you have the airline employees who handle your bags. They can tell just by picking it up. Then you have the guys working the X-ray machines, and the guys there helping or handling the bags. You have the guys driving the baggage carts, and the guys loading the plane.

If you don't have all these people in on it, you can have a problem. This was a country of snitches and informants. Beware because no one had anything else to do but pay attention to everyone else's business. So if the customs agent who was fixing our exit had it all set for 2:00 p.m., he might have had a short window with everything in place. Then in a moment, it can change, and he can no longer be able to do it.

My guys were finally told they could go home, but they had to report to the police station and were escorted to the airport and all the way to their seats on the plane. They were then given their passports.

Once they got home, I was finally able to sit down with Antonio and Eddy. They weren't angry or agitated; they were both pretty easy on me. First, I spoke to Tono, and he told me it was really terrible; the place was an old Spanish fort, probably built three hundred years ago or more. It was old and smelled, and the cell was very dark and damp.

He told me they first started in on Eddy. They would pull him out of the cell at all hours of the day and night. They could never tell if it was day or night. They weren't allowing them to sleep well and be rested and stronger. No, they were waking them every few hours and questioning them.

He told me that the gay guy, Luis, would cry all day, and he would ask himself over and over, "Why did I get involved, for a stupid fuckin' plane ticket?" Antonio told me he's sure Eddy told them everything. At first, he would hear Eddy's screams, but later Eddy would be returned to his cell after interrogations with a "prize" like something to drink. All three of them were questioned. I'm sure my name was mentioned more than once.

I was told that Eddy had eventually been taken on a ride to show them the building we had been to and identify some of the people we had bought cigars from. Eddy, of course, denies everything. He acts like Don Corleone. Antonio started referring to him as Eddy Corleoni. It was very funny because Eddy didn't look anything like a gangster or tough guy. He looked like a bookworm or an accountant.

They both told me I shouldn't be in any type of hurry to go back to Cuba: "If I were you, I wouldn't go to Cuba."

I asked them about my $1,200 that Capi returned, and they said, "Well, when we got out of jail, we said, 'Fuck Scott, we are going to dedicate the next few days of fun to Scott, because he's paying for it all.'"

As much as it hurt me to hear that my money was also gone, I had nothing to say. It was the least I could do for what they went through for me.

SOMEBODY

This was a major catastrophe. I lost a lot of cigars, which equals money. I lost suitcases, all the travel expenses, and more. This probably set me back $25,000, plus the prior trip with my wife; in total, I probably took a $30,000 beating.

So many thoughts were going through my head: Was it all my fault? Was I just too greedy? I knew if I just wanted to go to Cuba and fuck some girls, bring home a few boxes of cigars, and pay for my trip, that was pretty simple, but too petty for me, though. Hell, so many guys were starting to do that; the guys who just ride the tiny wave are content making a few bucks and having fun, trying to be like everyone else, and be players in the game of life. I just wasn't built that way; I couldn't see myself being like that. If I was going to do it, it was going to mean something.

I can't lie…I did suffer. I thought about "throwing in the towel," quitting, and giving up…but I didn't.

I think one of the strongest motives that I had drove me: I was a man on a mission. I didn't want to just make a living and have a good little business. I wanted more. I wanted to build a real life, a real business. I wanted to be one of those people I saw from a distance my whole life.

I wanted to be a *somebody*, a legitimate somebody. I had already been a street somebody, a criminal somebody, but it's not real, and it's not everlasting. The family that owns the business, the businessman, the entrepreneur, these people had a voice and a vote.

One of the worst feelings, in my opinion, is to know you don't have a voice or a vote; you don't fucking count. You are a nobody. Yeah, you can try to fool yourself, but you don't have shit to say about anything. The first step is education; that's your first step toward being someone. Education gives you a little voice and a little vote. Fame, too, will increase your percentage slightly. Money, boy, that's the one that makes what you have to say weigh something, and your vote gets important too.

There's a big but, though. You have to develop, too, as a human, a person, a man. You must fit the role. You have to carry yourself well, speak well, and when you can speak well and you are educated, you can actually defend yourself. Then the doors open (without having to kick them in). But it also needs to be legal. Sure, many people admire the bad guys, but don't really want to have anything to do with them on a personal level.

I was going to build that life. I had decided it, claimed it, made a promise, and was going to fulfill it. I had been working really hard for a few years before I started with the cigars, but I didn't move forward very much. I had managed and trained boxers, I sold the boxing gear from Mexico in Chicago, and I had become the one and only distributor of Century Martial Arts Products in all of Mexico. I had my own gym, and I gave group and private martial arts classes. I had an income, but I wasn't breaking any world records, and I didn't want to do anything illegal either.

Around that time, a few people had called me in Mexico asking when I was coming back to Chicago, and they were putting in orders or putting a claim on what I told them I had. This was something else that kept me going. I didn't yet have a lot of customers, and most of them were just working guys, but I could feel something better was coming.

I had learned a lot, and I had already been through a lot. Most people couldn't have handled even one day of this bullshit, but I could. I had to keep going. I didn't have anything else that had the potential this had, so I had to continue. I would make some changes, and I had to smooth out some of the details and get better.

I started packing for another trip. I decided this time I was going to take it all. I packed up every cigar from my humidor. I went through the whole process of wetting the bottom of the box, shrink-wrapping it, and carefully packing the suitcases. This took me a few nights to get it all done. Again, I loaded the room from floor to ceiling with the suitcases.

I was ready to go again. That's where I came back to, every time, no matter what happened: ready to go again. There wasn't any other option.

Chapter Nine

THE BEGINNING OF FACTORY CIGARS

I WAS AT A CROSSROADS IN MY CIGAR BUSINESS. I COULDN'T go to Cuba myself, and my humidor was running low. My friend Elier was also in trouble in Cuba and couldn't travel either. We were both stuck, trying to figure out our next move. A few people were bringing boxes back from Havana, but not nearly enough to meet my needs.

Some Mexican contacts were also bringing in cigars, but they were charging three to four times what I was used to paying in Cuba, and their stuff was garbage, a bottom-of-the-barrel product. Mexicans, especially the old-school types, often buy based on price alone; the cheapest wins. I bought a few boxes from them now and then, but only if something caught my eye. And even then, I inspected every detail before handing over a peso.

I finally talked my wife into going to Cuba for me. I set up a trip for her, her aunt, and her aunt's partner. I handled everything—flights, hotel, airport transfers. I even arranged a private driver in Havana. I wasn't about to send my wife on some shady mission digging through back alleys for black market cigars. She wasn't going to meet my usual street contacts. This was going to be clean and legit.

I sent her to the Partagás factory and told her to speak with the director, Ernesto López. I had called ahead, told Ernesto I was a friend of Larry's, and that my wife would be stopping by. She had a list of preferred brands and sizes and spent about a week in "basic training" with me before the trip.

She didn't need to be nervous. She'd be buying directly from the factory, and I assured her there wouldn't be issues at the Havana airport. I booked their return flight straight from Havana to Guadalajara, bypassing customs in Mexico City completely. I stayed home with our two small daughters (and the nanny) while she flew out.

The trip was just three days. She had the cash and the instructions. While she was there, we talked a few times by phone. Cuban calls were strange; every single one was monitored. The line would cut out if both people talked at once. You had to speak…pause…let the other person talk…pause…back and forth like that. It was awkward, but it worked.

She met with Ernesto, but he told her there was no stock available at the Partagás factory. Instead, he sent her to the cigar shop at Marina Hemingway, where a fresh shipment had just arrived. She took the thirty-minute drive and met the shop manager, Jorge.

Cigar shops in Havana were scattered all over. Small places were set up mostly for tourists and the "Habanos" brand. Nearly all of them had a master roller stationed at a table, hand-rolling cigars on-site. These unbranded cigars came without rings, boxes, or names—just raw craftsmanship. If you bought them in bulk, they came in bundles of twenty-five called *masos*. I would eventually buy a lot of these; they were high-quality, easy to smuggle, and carried a low invoice value for customs.

When the day came, I went to pick up my wife and the aunts at the Guadalajara airport. I stood outside the arrivals doors scanning luggage tags and looking for Mexico City connections. Time passed, people streamed out, but there was no sign of them. My stomach dropped.

Had she been detained? Was the bag flagged?

I hadn't arranged anything ahead of time, thinking it would be low risk. Between the three of them, they only carried about seventy boxes. This was supposed to be a test run for buying directly from official factory sources. Finally, she walked through the doors. One look at her face, and I knew something was wrong.

One of the bags hadn't made it to Guadalajara. Customs in Mexico City had held it. She had only one suitcase of cigars.

Fuck.

This business was so damn volatile. Nothing ever went as planned. I stormed back into the airport and tried to talk to customs, but they told me I'd have to take it up with the authorities in Mexico City.

Again—*fuck.*

It was already evening, and there was no point in pushing anything until the morning. We had one suitcase with about thirty-five boxes. Not a total loss, but disappointing. Back at home, we debriefed the whole trip. She told me how hard it was to get cigars from the factory, because tons of people were coming and going, all trying to buy. She said Jorge had been helpful and friendly.

Then I opened the bag.

And I realized, she didn't know cigars. Not really. She didn't know which brands were popular or what my customers were asking for. She did her best, and I appreciated that. Either way, this was it, my first batch of official, store-bought Cuban cigars.

The next morning, I hit the phones early, calling the Mexico City airport. Total nightmare. Dealing with any kind of government bureaucracy is tough, but in the third world? Multiply that by one hundred. I called a friend of mine, a comandante in the Federal de Caminos, and asked for a favor.

He drove into Mexico City from Puebla in his patrol car, pulled up right in front of the customs office, and walked in. The good news? The bag was there. The bad news? They weren't going to release it.

They gave him every excuse in the book. They said it was already documented, inventoried, and couldn't be touched. Their only "professional courtesy" was to return the bag to its origin: Cuba.

Fuck. Again.

They claimed they couldn't release it, but I knew how this worked. If I didn't intervene fast, the bag would disappear—"destroyed," on paper. In reality, someone would take it home or flip it for cash.

I thought about having it shipped back to Havana and paying someone there to pick it up at the airport. I made a few calls and considered the logistics. But it felt like a waste of time and energy.

So I decided I'd go to Mexico City myself.

I explained everything to my wife and told her to pack a bag, because she had to come too. The suitcase was under her name, and only she could claim it.

Mexico City is a monster of a city, both then and now. Even back in 1997, it was sprawling, chaotic, and dangerous. A concrete jungle packed with twenty-five million people, all fighting to get ahead, to eat, and to survive.

By that time, I'd already gotten used to passing through. Every trip to Havana meant connecting through Mexico City. I had my routine. A few contacts. Some restaurants I liked. A couple of decent hotels. I knew a handful of federales stationed in the city, a few boxing connections, and some hustlers I could trust.

But this trip wasn't for pleasure. I wasn't there to play jet-set. I was there to work. I was there to fight for that bag.

I was there to protect the business I was building—one box at a time.

MEETING CARLOS, THE BOSS OF CUSTOMS

My wife was Mexican—beautiful, sharp, and, truth be told, her looks often helped my cause. We headed to the airport around 11:00 a.m. I waited outside the customs office, watching. It wasn't located near the passenger terminals; it was way in the back, where all the cargo was handled. The scene was chaotic. People coming and going. Civilians just like me, all there with problems to solve.

I noticed a guy coming out—a Hasidic Jew, dressed in full

Orthodox attire—carrying a few cardboard boxes with the help of an assistant. I approached him. In Mexico City, people are cautious, and everyone's looking over their shoulder, but after a minute or two of small talk, I broke the ice. I told him my situation, and he nodded like he'd heard it a hundred times.

"They're as corrupt here as anywhere," he said matter-of-factly. Then he gave me the name of the top guy in charge of customs: Carlos. He told me to drop his name and say I was sent by him. I thanked him and went in alone.

Inside, I asked for Carlos. They told me to take a seat. I watched through the glass wall as an office assistant walked over to him. Carlos was already helping someone, and over the next hour, I saw at least four or five others come and go from his office. Finally, they called me in.

Carlos was young—maybe thirty-two—but he held serious weight. He was in charge of all the luggage, cargo, and packages at the largest airport in Mexico. That job came with power, and he wore it like a man who knew it.

He greeted me politely and asked how he could help. I explained the situation: one of our bags was held by customs. I handed him the claim check. He called for his assistant, who brought him the paperwork. He reviewed it, then looked up and said, "Ah...this is the same bag the comandante came to ask about."

He asked why I'd sent someone from the police. I told him I lived in Guadalajara, and having someone local check on it just made more sense. It was faster and cheaper.

He leaned back, thinking.

Then came the roadblock.

He said he couldn't release the bag because the claim check was under someone else's name. "I can't just give it to you," he said. "But if the person it belongs to is outside...have her come back after lunch."

I went outside, told my wife everything, and I was actually feeling hopeful. This might just work.

After lunch, I sent her in alone. I explained every detail and told her exactly what to say. Here's the thing: men in Mexican government offices might puff up with authority when dealing with other men, but a beautiful woman? They soften, bend, and practically melt.

About an hour later, she walked out with a suitcase.

Only it wasn't the same one that had been confiscated.

She explained: they had emptied our original suitcase, repacked the cigars into a different one, and said they'd be sending the original bag back to Cuba with something else inside. It was all part of the game. They needed to make it look official on paper.

But it had worked.

Carlos gave us his number and told us we could bring whatever we wanted through the Mexico City airport. The new deal? Two hundred and fifty dollars per suitcase. I finally had a contact for clearing Cuban cigars through customs in Mexico.

I was pumped.

It was now much safer and easier to buy cigars from the factory, get them out through Havana, and slide them into Mexico. But just because I had a customs hookup didn't mean the hustle got easy.

Let me be clear: switching from street cigars to factory cigars didn't make this a cakewalk. Not even close.

People think that just because there's a store inside the Partagás factory, it's like walking into a Costco. No way. That's not how it works in Cuba.

The factories had huge international contracts to fill—distributors from Europe, Asia, and the Middle East. Those orders got priority. Whatever was left might trickle into the retail shops. Might.

It was still a brutal hustle to get the boxes I needed.

I had to build relationships, grease palms, flatter egos, make side deals, and show loyalty with money. I had contacts all over Havana, from different stores, different managers, different inventory, all at different times. I was always on the move, hunting.

I'd show up at one shop, and nothing was available. They'd say, "Run to this other one, they just got a shipment," or "Come back in four hours." And I would. I'd haul ass all over the city, all day, all week.

Some days I found nothing.

Other days? Maybe a single box.

And then once in a while...I hit a goldmine.

You never knew. It was a game of luck, timing, and hustle.

Every store had its own little web of relationships. They had to keep everyone happy—brokers, fixers, regulars, and friends of the factory. They gave out little pieces of inventory here and there to keep the tips and favors flowing.

The truth? Most of those employees didn't have much control over anything. They earned maybe eight dollars a month. Most of them didn't give a shit about cigars or the international craze surrounding them. They weren't cigar lovers. They were survivors.

And me?

I was the crazy foreigner, sweating in the Havana sun, running through alleyways with a cell phone, a wad of cash, and a dream, chasing boxes of tobacco like they were bricks of gold.

Because in a way...they were.

I'LL BE BACK

Since I had been warned not to go to Cuba by several people, I heeded their advice. I didn't return to Cuba for a while. It seemed to me to be a long time. I had grown accustomed to Cuba, and I felt at home there, although it wasn't my home.

I decided to grow a beard. I thought it might change my appearance a little and maybe throw them off a bit. They would know me as a youngish, fit, clean-cut guy. I would at least "appear" different with a beard. Finally, I decided it had been long enough. I got a group of guys together, and off to Cuba we went.

I was nervous to arrive. I didn't know what to expect; I knew I wasn't involved with anything terrible, just some simple cigar running. As I waited in line to get to the immigration booth, so many thoughts went through my head: *What will they ask me? How should I answer?* Finally, it was my turn to face immigration.

It was a young woman. She looked at me and at my passport, smiled, and mentioned the beard. I just smiled and told her it was in honor of Fidel. I then ran my hand along the beard from my chin down. This was often how Cubans referred to Fidel without mentioning his name. She smiled, stamped my immigration card, and I was now inside Havana, Cuba.

I felt like I had a new lease on life. I was back in the game with a whole new energy.

FACTORY CIGARS

Around that time, I also connected with Papito, a guy who was a roller at the Partigás factory, and rolled the Double Coronas. These are a large cigar, approximately eight inches long, with a fifty-ring gauge. He was a level eight roller, which is expert level. During one of my many tours of the Partigás factory, I saw him and we made eye contact. I felt that he wanted to talk, so I waited for him to get out of work. I waited outside the factory and watched as the employees streamed out at quitting time.

Papito was just a peasant. He was uneducated, poor, very thin, and had a beard, like many Cuban men. It was similar to the beard that Fidel Castro had. I waited across the street. This way, I could not only see the door as they exited, but I could see for twenty feet into the hallway of the building. I saw him coming before he was at the door. I wouldn't have to spring into action at the last moment. He saw me when he approached the door; he was calm, but I could see the fear in his face.

He walked out and turned to his right as he walked. I mirrored him on the other side of the street. We simultaneously walked on opposite sides of the street for about two blocks. He was beyond scared. I finally crossed the street and approached him. We shook hands and started talking. He constantly looked around and told me he was worried that a coworker might see him talking to a foreigner.

I told him I was interested in buying his cigars rolled at the factory.

That's when he explained that both he and his wife worked as rollers at the factory, and they were allowed three cigars per day per person. I told him to accumulate them, and I would buy the *masos* every time I came. Between the two of them, they could accumulate a few boxes a month, and that could be a nice income for him.

Just to put things into perspective, he made about five dollars per month from his salary. I would pay him about twenty dollars per twenty-five cigars that he accumulated and saved for me.

He gave me his address and the phone number of his neighbors. It was common in Cuba for people to use the phones of any neighbors who had the luxury of having a phone line. I felt good. I felt like I was going to help someone make their life a little better. He was very poor and not too smart either. I suggested to him that maybe he could also recruit someone else from the factory, buy their few cigars that they were allowed to. He said he didn't want to talk to anyone and didn't want anyone else to know what he was up to. He was nervous, so I didn't push too much. I planned to go to his house and talk to him there, where he could feel more comfortable.

Most of the Cuban people were scared. The government was in complete control. People just didn't want to get in trouble, and it was pretty easy to get caught up, so many people snitched on each other. Some thought it was the right thing to do, and they did it with pride. Others did it out of jealousy and envy. He could lose his job or worse, and his job was all he had at the end of the day.

IMMINENT EVOLUTION

As my smuggling operation evolved, I was changing right along with it. Since I'd shifted to buying cigars directly from government stores and factories, I no longer had to hide in the same way or move around with a whole crew to carry bags. The work was still difficult. I had to find the right cigars, in the right quantities, but the chaos and danger had diminished. I became all business, almost mechanical, and focused on the job.

With those changes came distance. I lost contact with Capi and Luigi, and that's when I met a man who would become my near-constant companion in Cuba: Jaime Gisper. From then on, I used him almost exclusively as my driver.

Getting cigars out of Cuba was still a challenge, and airport inspections were tightening all the time. But my invoices were in order, the cigars legitimate, and I knew that if anyone checked, the paperwork would back me up. That confidence made me bolder, and it also made me valuable to someone like Jaime.

MEETING JAIME

I first met Jaime in passing at a cigar shop. He was there with a Brazilian customer and a friend of his, Anderson. Jaime stood out; around six feet tall, white complexion, a full head of gray hair, a long face, and an air of curiosity that was impossible to miss. He had the habit of sitting back and pretending not to listen, but you could feel him taking in every word.

Jaime had been a devoted servant of the new Cuba when Fidel Castro took power. As a young man, he believed in the revolution with all his heart. Over the years, he'd held many positions within the government, always in roles of trust and responsibility. He knew people everywhere and understood how to move and shake within the system.

When I met him, he was retired from government work and driving foreigners for twenty dollars a day—not for the money alone, but because it kept him in the mix, meeting people and dealing with the small dramas that crossed his path. His wife, Marta, was also a retired government employee. Together they lived in a ground-floor three-bedroom apartment in Miramar, just a block from the beach. In Havana, Miramar was *the* neighborhood—embassies, diplomats, and the closest thing the city had to an upper class.

Jaime had two adult children, pirated cable TV with HBO and pay-per-view (almost unheard of in Cuba), and a lifetime of stories. He told me once about traveling as a government buyer to the Soviet

Union, Hungary, Poland, and the Czech Republic to purchase heavy equipment for Cuba. On one of those trips, a seller slipped him a note offering a massive bribe if he chose their products. Jaime refused. He told them to subtract that amount from the quote instead. Whether it was integrity or fear of a setup, it showed his old-school loyalty to the cause.

He also told me about going to the docks in the early 1980s and throwing food at Cubans boarding boats to Miami during the Mariel exodus. Back then, he was fully committed to the revolution. But over time, travel and reality wore on him. He'd seen the world outside and seen how Cuba had been left behind. By the time I knew him, part of him still clung to the ideals, but part of him knew the cause was lost.

Anderson, the man Jaime was with the day we met, became another friend of mine. White, sandy-blond curly hair, about six feet tall, smart, and like me, he was in the Cuban cigar smuggling game. He took cigars all the way to Brazil, selling to wealthy clients. He was picky about food, bold enough to walk into restaurant kitchens to make sure things were cooked "his" way, and always had a complaint about something in Cuba—even the women.

You see, for those poor souls who haven't had the luxury of traveling to Brazil, let me tell you, Brazil probably has the highest concentration of beautiful women in the world. Anderson was never impressed with Cuban women or the ease with which you could have them. Their persistence often wore on him. Depending on his mood, he might bed one, then just as quickly dismiss her. Afterward, he'd complain and remind us how much more beautiful the Brazilian women were.

When Anderson and I were in Havana at the same time, we'd often share Jaime as a driver. Over time, Jaime became more than a driver for us; he became the guy we trusted to handle things.

THE WHEEL MAN

Jaime drove me from one side of Havana to the other every day. He met my carriers, my friends, my women, and my cigar suppliers.

He ran errands, picked up and dropped off packages, waited outside during meetings, and sometimes even helped line up girls. He was smart, funny, and direct to the point of being blunt.

One time, a young girl we'd picked up asked Jaime why the police always stopped her. He gave her a slow once-over and said, "Because you look like a whore." She wasn't offended; she knew he was telling the truth. Short skirt, midriff top, high heels, small backpack; it was the uniform of a young Cuban prostitute.

Another time, Jaime got into a shouting match with a bus driver after traffic held us up. Jaime yelled out, "*¡Negro de mierda!*" A few blocks later, the bus caught up at a light, and the huge driver got out, heading toward our car. Jaime stepped out, called him *caballo* ("horse"), told him not to get mad, that it was just an old man's words. They both smiled, and it was over.

LIKE FAMILY

Jaime's home in Miramar became my base of operations. I'd get calls there, leave and receive messages, and sort out countless problems from his living room. He invited me for meals—fresh lobster tails he bought for a dollar apiece—because he hated seeing us "waste" money in restaurants.

I trusted him completely. I'd call him from home when I was away, and sometimes send him to check cigar stores or factories to see if my orders were ready. He cared about me, about Anderson, and about a few other clients he considered friends. He never stole from anyone. He was a man's man.

I even watched the 1997 Shannon Briggs vs. George Foreman fight live on HBO at his house—a small thing, but in Cuba, having outside cable like that was almost impossible. That was Jaime: connected, resourceful, and always willing to open his world to us.

Jaime was so much more than a driver. He was a great man, and by the time my smuggling career ended, he was family.

DOCTORATE IN LIFE

I met Johnny D. through Eric. Eric often bragged and spoke highly of Johnny D. Johnny was the only male child of an old-fashioned Greek father, an old-school immigrant who made it big. Big to me anyway; the father had been a McDonald's franchisee. He accumulated eighteen McDonald's restaurants. So when his father passed away, he got six of the locations, his mother and sister got six each, too, and Johnny was in line to get his mother's six locations soon, because she was getting older and having a hard time managing them.

He was a colorful character, and he had the personality of one of those kids who had always had everything. He was probably spoiled and told he was the best since he was a child. Eric often said that the only thing bigger than Johnny's mouth was his heart. He was a good guy, and he was very cool to me. I hung out with Johnny a lot. He loved to brag and show off, and he lived in a good-quality suburb west of Chicago. It was the first time I had ever heard the term "sleeper house." He explained to me that the house looked smaller and simpler from the outside than it did on the inside. Once inside, the house opened up into a small mansion. He drove the largest, most expensive BMW.

At the same time, there was an incredible boom for the McDonald's toys "Beanie Babies." McDonald's sure picked up on how stupid people are and got right on board and threw fire on the flame. They started making unique and hard-to-find Beanies and limited editions. This made it even more wild.

Johnny had them all; he had everything and all of them. He took me upstairs into his attic and showed me his private accumulation of years and years of McDonald's toys and souvenirs. He had a massive amount of this collectible crap. I was impressed by the sheer quantity. He saved all the displays, too, and those were special, the acrylic cases with all the Beanies ever made. He was constantly throwing bags of Beanies at me (he was extremely generous). He didn't really give a shit, either, but he was smart enough to know that someday all this stuff would be worth big money. To this day, I still have a large bag of Beanies he gave me. I had thrown them into a closet and never looked at them again until recently. I looked them up online, and the ones that I have are currently worth a few grand minimum.

He had a live-in maid whom he paid $500 a week, with all food and board included. His finished basement also had a full guest apartment where she lived comfortably.

He invited me to his country club a few times, and I brought my friend Tono there once too. It was the Medinah Country Club in Medinah, Illinois. This is how the other half lives. It was spectacular to me. Once, he invited me there to shoot skeet. It was a first-class setup, and they kissed his ass. He was a championship-level skeet shooter. I was surprised. I thought I could shoot, but he blew me away, and everyone else there too. I watched him in awe; his technique was like a pro, and his posture was like something I had never seen before. He sort of leaned into it and didn't miss even one shot.

This was the life of a rich kid. He was confident and comfortable. He was raised so much differently than I was; I could see the difference, and I could even feel it. Even though I was tough and smart, I understood that this was the way I wanted my kids to be. It was a good road to be on.

Johnny was a good customer. He always bought between $5,000 and $10,000 in cigars, and he gave a lot of them away. He also introduced me to a few good customers. Johnny liked to play hard too. He drank, gambled, and did coke. He told me he had almost gone broke doing coke and chasing women, and had spent millions in just a year. That's when his family did some type of intervention.

I just sat there listening and feeling pain. Here I am building my life by smuggling cigars across the world, and this lucky idiot is wasting millions.

I thought for a moment that I would have been better off being his coke dealer than his cigar dealer. He sat there and told me he gave millions to his coke dealer in that period of time, but he was mostly better now. He then told me that he had cancer, and had been fighting it for a while now, and admitted he thought he got cancer from all the coke he had done. His cancer was in remission, and he was reluctantly living a much healthier lifestyle than before.

Here I was working my ass off to improve myself and my life, and this guy had it all and wasn't happy. I guess the difference is in the way you get it. He was given everything since birth; he didn't work for it or earn it, and he didn't have to think deeply and invent.

One day, he asked me to take a drive with him to look at a business. We drove for about forty-five minutes to the south side of Chicago. We went to this large hamburger place; it was huge and full of people. We went in, ordered, and sat down. Johnny was looking around and began to ask me what I thought about the place. I asked why.

He said, "Look at the place; it's full, it's selling nonstop." He went on to share his idea that he wanted to open a place like this. He started telling me the numbers and how much money could be made with a place like this. I couldn't understand why a guy who had a bunch of McDonald's (and a lot of money) would want to open a hamburger joint. He told me that a place like this can make twenty times more than any of his McDonald's stores. He also wanted to feel free, to be out from under the thumb of corporate America.

This I understood. He wanted to be free; he was tired of the chain of command, and he knew he was just another one of their bitches. But he made a lot of money. He told me he could make about $220,000 from each one of his stores per year. To me, this was great money and a dream that was out of reach for me. It's not easy to get to this level of life, and even harder for a thirty-three-year-old felon.

At the time, I couldn't quite feel the changes in me, but I was learning from all of these guys. This was like a doctorate in life. To be around people like these was an experience. In many ways, I was learning and I was being taught. I didn't really notice it at the time, but it was happening. I was learning and evolving throughout this process. I was becoming the businessman I wanted to be and getting closer to the life I wanted.

Chapter Ten

THE CIGAR GUY

I REACHED THE TOP LEVEL OF WHAT I COULD DO SMUGGLING and selling cigars, but that was never my end goal. This was the period in my life when I started to see what I really wanted and to see that I would eventually get out of the cigar business.

PREPPING FOR A TRIP TO THE BORDER

I was excited to get ready for the upcoming run to the border. Each cigar box needed its official import sticker—big ones, about three by five inches—and I had to peel and place them one by one. They all had to line up in the same spot to look uniform. It was slow work, but worth it.

Then came the packaging: small Ziploc bags with damp cotton balls for humidity, shrink-wrapping each box, sealing it all up. I loaded the finished boxes into suitcases and my backpack. I still had some leftover boxing gear in my inventory, so I packed that too. I figured I should get it to the US and sell it while it still held value.

I'd just bought a new Dodge pickup in Mexico: burgundy, clean, almost new, with oversized tires and sharp rims. It looked good, maybe too good. Once everything was loaded, the truck looked packed and way too obvious. You could tell it was hauling cargo from a mile away.

I had been working nonstop and hadn't found the right moment to make the trip, but customers were calling and waiting. A few of them were now selling cigars through me and making real money. I had to go.

One night around 11:00 p.m., I said, *Screw it. Just go.* I was already tired, but I jumped in the truck and started the drive solo. First stop: a big gas station near the toll road entrance just outside Guadalajara, then the road that would eventually carry me to Reynosa, across from McAllen, Texas.

I filled the tank and paid in cash—always cash. I never left without a decent stash on me. I needed it for tolls, food, gas, bribes, and emergencies. Between the cigars and boxing gear, I had about $20,000 worth of product in that truck.

As I pulled slowly out of the gas lane, double-checking everything in my mirrors, I noticed a man lingering nearby with his back to me. He was standing where he shouldn't be, too close, not doing anything, and I caught something in his body language. His hand wasn't at his side. He was fiddling with something.

I felt it, that street instinct, the one that kicks in seconds before something goes down.

I slipped the truck into reverse and paused.

Then he turned.

And pulled a gun.

He raised it toward me. I was about to get jacked. But I beat him by half a second.

I floored it backward.

The truck peeled out fast in reverse, tires throwing gravel and dust. Everyone at the station turned to look. He didn't fire. I think I surprised him more than he surprised me. I had spotted that twitch in his hand and sensed the setup. That tiny edge saved me.

I had enough room behind me, and the place wasn't busy. I kept reversing until I could whip the truck around. No way he was catching me on foot.

Robberies like that were common in Mexico—carjackings. And I was a prize: a shiny new truck, a packed load, and cash in my pocket. In those days, it was easy to swap plates and disappear a vehicle into a mountain town where no one asked questions. Guys would drive them until the wheels came off.

I aborted the trip on the spot and headed back home. I was wired but exhausted.

I had no cell phone back then. They weren't common yet, and the cost of calls was brutal. When I walked in, my wife was surprised to see me. I told her what happened and said I'd head out again the next day.

The next period of my life was spent learning and stepping up to the next level. I met amazing people who gave me a new sense of who I was and what I might be capable of.

WATER AND CIGARS DON'T MIX

It went on and on like that: getting the cigars, packaging and storing them, crossing the border any way we could, and selling them and starting it all over again.

One of the worst moments was when we were in another shitty hotel in another Mexican border town, and I was yet again waiting for Ramiro to show up with my cigars.

I was woken by banging on the door. Ramiro was outside. I opened the door, and he started to pass me bags. They had two cars directly outside my room with the lights on at 4:30 a.m. This can cause attention and wake people up. They passed me the bags fast and steady. I would just catch them midair at the doorway, turn around, and softly stack them wherever there was room. Ramiro and I barely exchanged words. We just went to work fast.

When he gave me the last bag, he just turned around and was gone.

All the guys got into their cars and were gone. The whole thing didn't take more than two minutes.

I would always be a little strung out on adrenaline after these types of events and would have a difficult time winding down and going back to sleep, but for now, I needed to rest. I went back to bed. I was just starting to relax, my mind was finally slowing down, and my body was too. I was in and out of consciousness when all of a sudden, my brain kicked in, and I was 100 percent awake. I had a revelation, a thought, a jolt of super urgency that ran through my body. I went from a state of grace to a state of panic in five seconds.

I first sat up to get my bearings and thought, *What was it? What hit me? What was going through my mind and body?* I sat there in the bed for a moment trying to put together the pieces, and then it hit me. *Bang!* I jumped to my feet, and I was 100 percent awake and aware of what it was. At that moment, I knew it was urgent and an emergency.

I realized I had felt humidity or water when I was handling the bags. Something was wet. Wet and cigars don't go together. Cigars and water are an emergency.

The room was still almost dark, with just a little light showing through the almost transparent, crappy curtains on the window. I immediately reached for the bags. I started to feel them, touch them, hoping I was wrong. I wasn't wrong. There was water—a lot of water.

I was now in salvage mode. I turned on the lights, and my wife woke to see me moving fast. She could tell something was very wrong by the way I was moving and my attitude. I was first trying to separate the wet bags from the dry ones. I wanted to minimize, control, and reduce the damage. The bags that were 100 percent dry were separated into one area. Then I separated the very wet from the least wet bags. I also had to keep them apart from each other to keep the spread under control.

I unpacked bag after bag with urgency. Some of the bags were soaked, and others were not so bad. I didn't have time to waste. I just kept unpacking and separating.

I wasn't happy. Here I am at 5:00 a.m., awake and watching my investment slip through my hands. I'm looking at the damage. I'm looking at so many boxes of top-quality, factory-bought, pristine, and highly sought-after Cuban cigars that are trashed.

I finally had all of the bags emptied and the boxes separated with a method to the madness. I now began to remove the plastic wrap. I sometimes felt terrible; all my work looked to be lost and wasted. As I removed the plastic, I could see water just pouring out of the plastic, which meant the boxes had been exposed to a lot of water. I kept up the ferocious pace and pushed forward, opening and unwrapping, separating and classifying.

I had all of the boxes that seemed to be fine without any moisture in the bathroom. I had a huge pile of bags in one corner, and the rest of the room was literally covered with boxes of Cuban cigars...there was a small mountain of stretched, wet, and used wrapping too. The room looked like some type of manufacturing was going on. I took a moment to think, and then I took off for the hotel office.

It was about 8:00 a.m., and I had no time to waste. I started knocking. They quickly answered and could see the urgency on my face. I told them I needed another room immediately. They had both rooms on either side of my room vacant. I got the keys to both rooms, and I told them we'd work out the details later.

I ran to the rooms and opened them both. I turned the air conditioning on full blast, left the doors open, and started transferring boxes to the other rooms. I just needed room to spread them out and groom them. My room was so full of cigar boxes that I couldn't move, and I couldn't do what I thought needed to be done. I needed to spread them out, open the boxes, leave them open, and keep them separate so the humidity didn't transfer and get worse.

I had remembered that in the Cuban cigar factories, they had a "cold" room where they stored all the cigars after they were collected from the rollers. All cigars were put into the cold room for a while before sending them off to the rest of the processes. This is what I would have to do too. I started opening boxes, and it was even worse than I thought. Many boxes were wet and damaged all the way through. The cigars were wet, too, the boxes were wet, and some had already started to fall apart.

I soon had three entire rooms full of cigars; they were literally *everywhere*. I had them spread all over the rooms: the floor, beds, tables, counters, and dressers. I went from room to room rotating, moving, checking, and fixing everything.

After many hours of this, the adrenaline finally wore off, and I got one more additional room, without cigars all over the place, and I fell dead asleep. I was completely exhausted. I had been running on survival instincts for about eight hours, and I finally had a type of control over the situation. Many hours before I had accepted the disaster and faced it head-on, I saved what I could. I did all I could do to minimize the loss.

I woke up a few hours later, and I was starving. I remembered the cigars as soon as I woke and immediately just came to attention and went to the other rooms. The sun was very bright and hot. I squinted and waited for my eyesight to adjust. As I entered the first room, I was again blown away by the sight. The room was filled with cigars. It was impressive, an entire room loaded out with cigars: stacks, piles, and boxes everywhere. To almost anyone, especially a broke cigar smoker, this was impressive. To my surprise, the cigars were doing okay, the water was mostly gone, and the boxes themselves were drying. Everything looked stable.

I went to a phone to call Ramiro. He told me it was raining and that the river had risen. He said one of his guys lost his balance to the current and started to be taken away, and came close to drowning. He said they really struggled to make this trip; the guys had even dropped bags into the water, where they got submerged completely. He apologized but told me there was nothing he could do; it was out of his control, but at least they didn't lose anything, and no one got hurt.

So this now painted a much clearer picture for me. I had suspected something like this had happened.

I continued tending to the cigars for the next few days. I rolled them over, I adjusted their positions, and I just kept at it throughout the days. I cleaned out the trash, I salvaged any of the boxes that I could, and trashed the rest. I was able to separate more boxes that appeared to be dry and safe. I did lose a lot of boxes. There were quite a few boxes and cigars that were a total loss, but not as many as I'd feared.

Eventually, the time came to meticulously inspect the product. I had to find all the damage and imperfections before I sent the cigars on their way. I wouldn't have the space once they arrived at my mother's apartment. I had to get everything straight here and now; I also couldn't afford for my customers to find *any* of the imperfections on their own.

It was unbelievably difficult for me, since these had become my "pride and joy." This was my first load of factory-bought cigars. I had worked so hard to get to this point. I had been building up my business, doing everything I could to make it the best I could, and something like this happens.

One thing I learned from my cigar days: making and building a life isn't easy. It's not for the soft or weak. I had one problem after another, and I just kept moving forward, finding solutions or making them up as I went along.

As I began my inspection, I had the doors to all three rooms open, and I went from room to room, separating and grading. I would inspect each box first on the outside, and then I would flip, roll, and rotate all the boxes to make sure that the outside of the box was intact, with no water spots, no swelling, no cracking, no visible damage, or signs of imperfections. It was like someone who would look at a diamond; I would even take different angles to see everything, rotate them at different points, and move my body around like a dancer, making sure to see everything from every possible angle and in all different lights.

Eventually, I had everything back under control. I had one room full of boxes that were still perfect, and room number two with boxes that were also fine but just not pristine. I had the third room with the worst of them.

The one thing I was sure about was the humidity. Even though I had kept them out of the box and spread them out well, some of the cigars were still wet or moist.

I just couldn't stay there forever. I had to get them shipped and get myself to Chicago.

I had already lost about 10 percent of the load. What I had to throw away in my hotel room at the border was already a lot, and I didn't want to lose more. I had worked so hard to salvage as much as possible, and I had cut my losses greatly by acting fast. If I hadn't noticed the wetness of the bags as they were passed to me, or if I was just lazy and let it pass because I was tired and wanted to sleep, or if I was just plain stupid and didn't pay attention, I might have lost it all. It could have been catastrophic, a total loss. The water would have gone from box to box and cigar to cigar; the loss would have probably ended my run as a cigar smuggler.

When I finally slowed down and came out of the zone, I was exhausted. I noticed that my wife was just staring at me. I smiled and asked her, "What?" She had never seen someone go into a zone and work like that ever before in her life.

She asked me, with all of the bad stuff that has happened since I started this cigar thing, "How can you keep doing it?"

I don't know. I guess I just wanted so much to have a good life, I was willing to work as hard as needed and make sacrifices that others won't or can't make. The truth is, I just didn't stop to feel sorry for myself. Sure, I had moments when I felt I was done, but I would rest and just keep going, no matter what happened.

I sent the boxes and made my way to Chicago again, where I would have to wait for my boxes to arrive from UPS. I could only hope that the cigars arrived without having problems from the water issue. I was worried about the several different problems that could be secondary effects of them getting wet. Mold could build and form, and this could make the cigars look bad if there were visible signs on the cigars. It could spread from cigar to cigar; it could become a white spot, a white powder stain on the cigar that just won't wipe off. Some people get very intoxicated when they smoke a cigar with mold; most never know what happened or why. They just wonder if they felt ill because of the cigar.

All cigar tobacco has dormant eggs too. The cigar beetle (*Bichos*) can hatch with the dampness, and if you add heat along the journey, it becomes more likely.

The cigars could swell and pop the outside wrapper and rip through the bands. The ends could spread and start to look ragged, the color of the cigars could change. Many negative things could happen, and the trip could be the catalyst.

But right now, all I could do was wait and hope for the best.

Finally, the cigars arrived. There were no real signs of problems. I made sure to unpack everything. The living room and dining area of my mother's apartment looked like a cigar factory for a moment.

Like always, I was impressed to see this sight: more than three hundred boxes of fine Cuban cigars spread out in a small room. It resembled a factory.

I finally finished everything, I got rid of the trash, and packed up all the bags again. After all the hard work and stress, I was finally winding down. I took a cigar out of the large Ziploc bag that I had put them into. It was a Romeo & Julieta Churchill, factory-bought and recently river-soaked at the Mexican border.

I went outside onto the balcony, where the weather was fresh but not cold. I sat down by myself and lit the cigar. To my surprise, it was very good. It was at one time very wet, one of the worst. It burned well, and it had a good taste, fresh, better than normal. Amazing.

Now that all the backroom work was done, I could finally start selling again.

GET ME OUT OF HERE—PLEASE

When I was in Cuba, I always bought cigars from a guy named Jorge, and he would sometimes help by calling other stores to see what they had, and he would make sure that Andrea would roll my special cigars too. He was the manager of the cigar store in the Marina Hemingway; it was a respectable store. Jorge lived with his mother just a block away from the Partigás factory, in an old, rundown building.

We often went to his apartment to socialize and hang out. On one of these visits, he confided in me, "I need to get out of Cuba." I asked him if he was asking me for help, and he said yes.

This was something new to me. I didn't know much about it since I had never been involved with the process. I told him I would look into it. I had known at least twenty Cuban women who had gone through the process, but all of them married a foreigner to get out.

I could feel an urgency in Jorge. He was stiff and uneasy. I asked him what was going on. He confided that his brother-in-law was in big trouble. He was caught stealing at one of the cigar factories, and they found $8,000 in his apartment. Jorge was worried because he vouched for him, and they might now take a look at Jorge. All the people in this industry were stealing. They couldn't live on their salary. Jorge made about fifteen dollars per month plus tips. Actually, he made all of his money through tips.

Once I got home, I told my wife what Jorge confided in me. I told her that I felt like I owed something to someone. I was making a good living off Cuba and felt I needed to give back. Jorge hadn't done anything special for me, but I didn't really have anyone else who asked me either.

Because of Jorge, I met a Cuban woman in GDL, Niurka. She was an attorney in Cuba and also practiced in Mexico. She was a strange little woman, small, skinny, and not very attractive. She was probably fortyish and had been living and working in Mexico for a few years. Niurka would help me do everything to get Jorge out. She had done it many times before too. Not only did she help Jorge to get out of Cuba, but I was also able to introduce her to many other families who would then be able to get their families out too.

Niurka had a sister living in Cuba, and she still worked for the government as an employee of Fidel Castro; she was also his friend. Her sister was a prominent government psychologist who was well-respected within her group. She had pictures throughout her house of her and Fidel together at many different places and times.

She was helping us with some of the requirements needed for Jorge's paperwork. The process was time-consuming and complicated. We spent a lot of time with her while going through the process. When you spend time with someone, you build trust or at least a comfort zone.

One evening, I was at her house with her family, and we went outside on the ground-floor porch in the front of the house. We sat chatting and watching the people walking and shuffling about. While talking, she asked me if I had studied psychology.

I smiled (because I knew why she asked), and I said, "Kind of, why?"

When I was a teenager, I had a very close relationship with the psychologist from my school and spent a lot of time with her. This led me to feel like I was also a psychologist. I even thought I, too, wanted to study to become a psychologist, but I never did. Oddly enough, I did have a good understanding of life and people, and I could relate to it well.

She told me that she sensed something about me that made her ask if I, too, was a psychologist. This was coming from a person who was well-educated in her field. I then told her that my young life had been a mess, and I said, "If I had grown up in Cuba, I would probably be in prison or dead."

She immediately contested my claim. "No, Scott, maybe you would be a general in the military or have a high-ranking position in government."

I had never looked at it that way. I never thought about my life that way. She said, "You are very intelligent, and if you had a different environment or upbringing, you have no idea what you could have been." She told me to stop thinking that way about myself. She said, "You are still young, and you need to forgive and forget your past and become the adult you were always meant to be."

These words are always on my mind. I have never forgotten what she said to me that night, and how it must have affected me so I still remember it to this day. It's sometimes these small things in our lives that can have a significant impact on our lives and future.

These words were part of the education I was getting, which was building me up for the next level in my life.

Chapter Eleven

FAKES

OFTEN, I GOT SCRUTINIZED OVER THE CIGARS. AS THE FAD rose, so did the scams and the fakes.

I had met a group of Cubans out of Miami who were making fakes. They were really putting a dent in the market and making a lot of money. It seemed like they were getting away with it, and I often wondered if they were given permission or forgiveness by the US government. They were damaging the Cuban cigar industry for sure. They did put a hurt on the Cuban government by doing this, so maybe they were CIA-affiliated.

A lot of guys thought they had a contact; they thought they were buying legitimate cigars from international websites or whatever, but most were fake. The cigars were just USA-made copies, or foreign-made but not in Cuba.

I decided to make a few video recordings in Cuba as proof, to at least demonstrate my presence in Cuba. I knew that most guys who sold Cuban cigars did not go to Cuba; they were just middlemen and hustlers. I was the real thing. I basically lived in Cuba for several years and honestly tried to get the best cigars I could find.

I filmed the operations of the Partigás factory, the stores, the streets, everything. I tried to keep it related to cigars as much as I could, because at the end of the day, my customers didn't care about the Cuban culture or their striving for freedom. They wanted cigars. The video was just a prop to help back up my claims. I knew they were really Cuban cigars; I knew that they were all from Cuba, but I had to prove it all the time. It was just always in my face. Over and over again, there was someone questioning and scrutinizing me and my cigars. It was often from a distance, someone who didn't even know me or buy from me, but they could really start some trouble with their know-it-all comments.

I went to Andrea at the Habanos store in the Marina Hemingway to film her specifically. She was shy and scared, and she didn't want to be on film. She had been a trusted personal roller for Fidel Castro for many years of her life, and now she finally had a job where she could make a living for herself and her family. I chased her around the store. She went so far as to run outside the store and hide; she was crying and scared for her life.

There was a time when she was under great scrutiny and security. She was strip-searched every day when she got to the Laguito factory. She was a Black woman with not much schooling and not much opportunity in Cuba. She didn't know what I wanted and why I would want her on film. I explained to her what was happening to me and about people accusing me that I was selling low-quality cigars and cheating them.

Some of the cigars that she specially made for me cost thirty dollars per cigar. I also had to make my orders in advance and be very patient. I couldn't get all I wanted and as much as I wanted. First, because they were expensive, $300 to $500 for a bundle (*maso*) of only twenty-five cigars. I finally convinced her that it was innocent, there was no danger for her, nothing political, and she would only say good stuff about her country. Finally, she gave in and let me film her working.

I filmed her rolling, and she showed us the tools she used and the cigars she had in the process, etc. I had her make a personal message to Michael Jordan (the story of how I started selling to him is later in the chapter).

I used my videos many times. Back then there weren't any social media platforms to share them on, so I would carry that recorder and all of its parts and cables around with me and either stand in a parking lot with a bunch of guys huddled around the small device and sharing a glimpse, or I would use the cables to connect it to someone's TV set and watch it on the big screen.

Either way, it worked. It started a lot of chatter and myth; anyone who saw it told ten other people about it and backed my claim of legitimacy. Most of these guys would never, ever be visiting Cuba, and this way, they got to see a little of the island and where the Cuban cigars they smoked actually came from.

The truth is that a cigar is a cigar. Even if we pretend that a Cuban cigar is the best, is there a noticeable difference between Montecristo and Romeo y Julieta? Absolutely not! All of my cigars came from Cuba. They were what they were: Cuban cigars.

I brought them the *image* that they wanted. I brought a good story and adventure into their lives. It was like bringing coke to them while they were in college. The dealer came to the door and brought them their contraband. I took all the risk, and they got to enjoy what they wanted at that moment.

Either way, the video was good enough for now to prove to the naysayers that it was legit and that I had the right product, authentic Cuban cigars.

A DIPLOMATIC BAG

I met Mary by accident. She also bought cigars from Rubio. Mary was the wife of an African diplomat. She had a diplomatic passport and lived in an official diplomatic estate. She was a middle-aged woman, black as coal, short and stout, and she wore African garb. She spoke French, Spanish, and some English. She talked like a typical African;

she basically yelled. She was all about the money. She was a hustler. She didn't fuck around, and she was fearless. She also smuggled cigars around the world. She was making money, and she put in the time.

I would choose the cigars from Rubio, and she would do the work of bringing them to Mexico for me. As always, I carefully scrutinized the products. I only had to do it the first time with Rubio because his product was flawless. He knew what I wanted and needed. He didn't fuck around and play games. He supplied the best of the best. The Cohiba brand came in an all-wood box with a nice varnish finish, high-quality clasps and hinges, and just a few stickers and logos.

I would meet him at Mary's home, and we would take care of business in one of the rooms. I had heard from several friends in Cuba that all the Africans were into something illegal to make money. We were sure the government knew what she was doing, but just let it slide. She had a diplomatic passport, and anyone who carries one is almost untouchable. It was only cigars, not like we were planning to kill Kennedy. We traveled together often, and she would just pass my cigars through customs in Cuba and then again in Mexico. Once we got that done, we usually each went our own way.

On one of our trips from Havana to Cancun, we were stopped in the airport by an inexperienced or new customs agent. We had about twelve suitcases between the two of us. The agent demanded to search the bags, but Mary refused. She told the agent that it was not allowed, but the agent insisted. Mary got radical. First, she was loud and a bit obnoxious, but now she was mad, and she didn't give an inch. Everyone in the airport was looking at us, and it was quite a scene. She dove on top of the mountain of bags and demanded the BOSS. "Bring me the *jefe*," she bellowed. There she was in the center of the baggage claim area, lying on the bags and making a huge scene.

The young agent didn't know what to do, but he stood his ground too. He didn't move. He had someone call the boss, and after half an hour, the boss showed up. It was very simple for the boss. He knew the law and the rules. He read the young agent the riot act and let her go. You can't do anything to the holder of a diplomatic passport, period.

It was amazing. It was so cool to watch, funny, and uncomfortable. I felt sorry for the young agent; he looked like an idiot and probably was. Mary and I did this for about a year. She would come all the way to Guadalajara to stay at my house and hang out for a few days. She would bring many of her own cigars, and I would help her by selling them to the local cigar guys. She wasn't greedy at all. She sold cheap and wanted to sell in volume.

Since I had done so many trips with Mary, and she had taken my bags so many times, I ended up with some of her travel bags. They all had her name written in marker all over the bags: Mary, Mary, Mary. I never really paid attention to it until one day I used her bags to load my cigars and go through customs in Havana. Like magic, my bags went through customs, no secondary inspection, no agents, no bullshit, nothing. Right then, I figured out that everyone knew her and stayed the fuck away from her, period. I used her bags often after that, and only once I saw that an agent came out of the back room and only gave a glance around the waiting area, and that was it. Her bags went right through security, with no questions asked and no scrutiny.

I didn't figure it out immediately. I noticed they didn't pull my bags and call me back to security for a search, but I wasn't going to go back and complain. I was a bit concerned. I wondered if something had happened. Did they steal them? Once I got to Mexico City and to the baggage claim, they were there. They were really ugly bags, just old, cheap quality, poor design, and a crappy pattern. The only thing obvious was they were marked with "MARY" or "MARI" with big ugly black letters. Then it hit me: they knew her and knew her bags. She probably had an issue with every customs agent in the country, and I'm sure she spread a few bucks around too. Once, she made a phone call to someone for me so my departure was all set up, and she didn't have to travel with me.

I took advantage of those bags for as long as I could! They were awesome, and they just made it less stressful. Because I never knew what to expect at the airport. At any moment I could have a problem; they could get a calculator and start to add up my invoices.

My invoices were always valued at least 50 percent less, sometimes 75 percent. I had to make last-minute deals, and many times, I would start to talk to them fast, confuse them, distract them, make jokes, drop names, whatever it took to get them off their objectives. I had business cards made for my wife. They were for a very big news company. She would say her father was the owner, and we would threaten to write about our bad experiences. I would have to try everything.

It was very stressful because, at the end of the day, it was up to them. They could detain us, we could be arrested, and the products could be confiscated. I always tried to give them money, a payoff, but I had to evaluate, and I had to think of ways to make the offer and have an escape if they were offended.

The process of bribing must be discreet and tactful. You must be very careful, too, because many people could take it the wrong way, and you could end up in jail.

I underwent a lot of changes during that time. It was like I was growing and maturing at the same time as the changes were being made. Since I was buying cigars from the government stores, I no longer had to hide the same way, and I didn't need to bring a lot of guys to carry bags anymore. Since the problems and the changes, I also didn't have contact with Capi and Luigi. I met Jaime and used him almost exclusively as my driver. Finding the right cigars and quantities I wanted was still hard and always would be, but the risk and disorder had diminished. I was all business and like a cyborg. It was also still challenging to get a large amount of cigars out of Cuba through the airport, and getting harder all the time.

Having the right people in my pocket helped a lot. But it was no guarantee, as I was about to find out.

BEST-KEPT SECRET

On one of my Cuba trips, I noticed that at the back of the waiting area of the airport, there was a small cigar shop. I had never really paid attention to it before. I had either not seen it or just didn't pay attention, since I hadn't been interested in the more costly factory cigars. It was all the way in the back of the airport waiting area, right next to the doors that we would line up for and exit to take the bus out to the airstrip to board our planes. It was old and dated, with almost no signage and no advertisement. Again, almost everything is owned by the state; that means run by the state. They just don't really care. There's no personal interest and no real experience in real business. Communist business is kind of like: take it or leave it.

I had a lot of time, and I walked over and started looking. Two young girls were working there, and almost all Cubans were easy to talk to and friendly. They were cute and easy to talk to; even though working with or around tourists was an advantageous position, they were still not corrupted. The display cases were made of old wood with glass tops and fronts, and contained almost no inventory. They had only a few boxes, and just the cheap stuff.

I started asking them questions, and they said they didn't really sell much, so they didn't really order much. I asked if they could get more if they wanted, and they said yes. One of the girls was the manager and had all the same contacts as any other store, and said she could request more and get it.

A bright light went off in my head! I asked her if there were any controls or limits on the amount a customer could purchase, and she said no. You were already past security and scrutiny, so you could buy anything and as much as you wanted.

I asked for their phone numbers, and they both gave me their numbers without hesitation. I told the manager to place an order, a big one. I gave her a list of what I wanted. I told her I would call her in a few days to confirm what she was able to order and get. I told her not to put it on display, to hide it in the storage cabinets for me, and I would take care of her. I gave them each twenty dollars in good faith and laughed and joked for a few more minutes.

I didn't want them to notice how excited I was, but I was glowing. This was huge for me, and the best part of it was that no one had thought of it yet.

I called the manager a few days later, and she told me she had put in the order and was waiting for the main office to respond. I told her to talk to Ernesto at the Partigás factory if she had any problems, and tell him they were for "Scott Mexico," which was what they called me.

I called her back a few days later, and she said they had approved her order and that she would get the cigars in about two weeks. I was already planning my return trip. I was so excited, like a kid on Christmas. To me, it was all about the end product: money. All the cigars meant to me was profit. I tried to squeeze the most juice I could out of each trip, box, and cigar.

This was my second chance at making real money to take myself to that next level in life, and I wasn't going to squander it. I never told a soul, especially not the factory store employees. Word would spread, other foreigners would swarm in, and the whole thing would get burned. Too many cooks ruin the broth. This was my best-kept secret, and I'd take it to the grave.

GRINGO AT THE GDL AIRPORT

Most people who knew me knew I was the cigar guy. Anything cigar-related—people buying, selling, asking about trips to Cuba, or even about Cuban women—I'd get the call.

One warm summer night in Guadalajara, Louie from the airport called me.

"Hey Scott, I got some American guy here at the airport. Customs just took his suitcases."

"Okay, and?"

"They were full of cigars."

"Say no more. I'm on the way."

I jumped in my car and headed toward the small, worn-down Latin American airport. Louie said it was a lot of cigars in big suitcases. He was already outside when I pulled up. He jumped in, and we cruised down the short road that looped around the terminal. We hadn't gone far when Louie shouted, "There he is!"

I spotted him. He was an uptight-looking American walking briskly, almost like he was trying to disappear. I slowed and rolled down the passenger window.

"Hey man," I said, "you got your bags taken?"

He looked over, eyes darting between me and Louie, trying to place us. He definitely recognized Louie from inside—maybe the uniform, maybe the airport employee badge—and I saw the panic flicker in his face.

Then, just like that, he bolted. Not quite a run, but damn close.

I nudged the car forward.

"Hey!" I called out. "We're speaking English. We're offering help here."

He slowed, then finally stopped. But he wouldn't really look at us. The guy was hunched over, spooked, and wouldn't give us a straight answer. To be honest, I started getting pissed. I thought about getting out and roughing him up a little. He looked like a total lightweight—nervous, soft, no street in him. I was basically there to take his shit, and if he'd had the bags with him, I probably would've taken them. One way or another. That was the plan.

What I needed now was information.

Where were the bags?

What kind of cigars were they: factory, store, or street?

How many boxes? How many cases?

I needed answers to figure out my next move.

He told me he'd been flying to Tijuana and had a layover in GDL. Customs flagged his luggage and pulled him off the plane. Now he was stranded here. All he wanted was to get back to the US. He was shaking, couldn't trust anyone, and probably saw me and Louie as two more people trying to hustle him, which we were, just with better manners.

Still, I got it. He was alone in a foreign country, had just gotten his shit seized by Spanish-speaking authorities, and now two random guys are chasing him in a car. But if he'd just talked, if he'd worked with me, he might've gone home with at least a portion of those cigars. Maybe. I can't lie. I might've kept them all. I was a street guy in remission, not rehab.

If he'd played it smart, I would've told him: We can help you recover your bags for a fee. I'd have gotten all the details: receipts, inventory, the whole setup. I could've gone in clean, spoken their language, paid the right guy, and walked away with the haul.

Instead, he kept speed-walking like we were trying to mug him. His look alone made me want to drag him out of his sneakers.

Eventually, I gave up on him and started thinking about the next move—the bags.

Where were they now? How could I get them?

I parked and went inside with Louie. He knew everyone at that airport. Within minutes, we were standing in the international arrivals area with the boss of customs. Right there, in his office, were the bags: six massive suitcases. Full of cigars.

I offered to buy them on the spot.

"Look," I said, "the guy's not coming back. He just wants to go home. I'm here to handle it. You can deal with me, someone who speaks your language, and make this easy."

The customs boss looked at Louie like, *Is this guy cool?* Louie gave the nod.

Some people might not get it. I wasn't building some everlasting business here. I was on a mission to make as much as I could, as fast as I could. That guy wasn't my friend. I didn't even know him. He was jungle prey, the same way I'd been to the guys who robbed me in Mexico City. I took advantage of the moment and paid pennies on the dollar for thousands of dollars in cigars. There was no drama, no paperwork, and no hassle.

The next thing you know, Louie and I walked out the front doors with six suitcases in tow, loaded with cigars for a bargain price.

THE LIST

I sold to so many people during this time. I'm not going to list all of them, but the list grew and grew, and eventually I was selling to some well-known people.

I had one good customer who didn't buy a lot of cigars himself but set me up with a lot of other customers. He was Italian (he had direct mob ties), and he was about fifty-five and the owner of a Toyota dealership (at that time, it was probably worth $10 million), but he was cheap. He introduced me to one of his nephews, who was just a salesman, and he spent ten times more money than his uncle did. Through both of them, I met at least ten other customers.

Through Dick and Gary, I met Ira, who was a unique character, very old-school. He had his office in an older, blue-collar, semi-industrial area of Chicago: Belmont and Western. This place was significant for several reasons. First, it was the location of the former Riverview Amusement Park from 1931 until it closed in 1967. More relevant to me, it was a notorious police station in the nineteenth district.

I had been a guest of honor several times; they had the area burglar squad, and I was once a renowned burglar. I was once kidnapped by them, questioned, interrogated, starved, beaten, and held for several days without food for an armored car robbery. I was never charged, and the case was never solved.

Ira ran an office that handled insurance claims that the insurance company didn't want to pay up or cover enough, and he battled them for a huge cut. His office was something out of an old movie, including a hidden door to a secret room. Like a small boy, he pulled out his small control and smiled as he pushed the button, and the hydraulic shelf unit opened. It was really cool and definitely not common or cheap.

Ira and I once had a debate about cigars and the reality of all the fakes going around, and he said, "How do I know for sure that yours are from Cuba?"

I said, "Because you're a smart man, and I come highly recommended."

He said, "Yes, I'm very smart and good at what I do, but I don't really know shit about Cuban cigars." He was right. Outside his office, illegally parked without any tickets or citations from the police or city, sat his brand-new beautiful Cadillac sedan with a very special license plate "0" (Zero) in the middle. He was a very close friend of George Ryan, the sitting governor of the state of Illinois.

I sold cigars to the governor several times, and I was invited to go with them to Havana in the late 1990s when they were organizing an "official" trip.

I would have served as a first-rate travel guide, but again, I was terrified they would check into my past, and I would be discovered as a former scumbag and banished from my cigar customer circle. I feared they would find out about *all* of my past. It wouldn't be very hard. So many of my customers were wealthy and influential; they could find out everything, and I always feared it.

I met a lot of the Chicago athletes too. The cigar trend was on the rise, and these guys were always in the mix.

I had recently been introduced to Shaun, a recently retired NFL player and a member of the 1984 Super Bowl champion Chicago Bears football team. He bought a few boxes, and we became friends. Shaun was a great guy. I met him through photographer Mark Hauser; they were good buddies. Eventually, it was Shaun who introduced me to Richard, 23, and many more professional athletes and several high-profile businessmen.

I had been selling to Shaun for a while. I usually went to his townhouse outside of Chicago in a suburb. One day, I showed up, and there were a few more cars than normal. Inside were several more guys; one of them was NFL great Richard. This was the first time I would meet Richard. He, too, was a member of the 1984 Super Bowl champions, the Chicago Bears. Shaun wasn't a real big guy (five foot eleven) for a football player, but Richard was a big guy (six foot five). Richard was nice to me immediately. We became friends and started hanging out soon after.

I started to sell to the Chicago Bears; the coach was Dave Wannstedt, and it was 1996. I was invited to the Bears' training facility out in the suburbs. I was taken right into the locker room. At first, I was there pretty much alone, but soon enough, the entire football team was there looking through my cigars. I had no problem getting my friend Stuart into the locker room. He got to enjoy hanging out with an NFL team in their locker room. We took some pictures, and I sold a lot of cigars that day. I sold to everyone, including the coaches, the players, etc.

I had been selling cigars and hanging out a little with Chicago player Donnell Wollford, running back, college standout, and first-round draft pick for the Chicago Bears. Donnell had lost his driver's license to a DUI, so he had a limo driver. Everywhere he went, he had the driver. I'm not sure, but I would guess the team made him get a driver to keep him out of trouble. Donnell was cool; he was a young football stud, having fun and taking advantage of what was offered. At that time, he was a local hero and a star player of a major sports team in Chicago. I went over to his suburban apartment a few times. He bought cigars as well, as he liked to hang out with me. He was cool to me.

This was a time in my life when I was going through some real changes. I wasn't much interested in bling and hanging out at the cool places. I was a man on a mission, and I was focused. Sure, I enjoyed some of my time while doing the cigars, but my future was my focus.

A few months later, I was in Vegas for the Tyson vs. Holyfield fight, and a bunch of the Chicago Bears were there too. I had been talking to Shaun a few times a day because they were trying to get a VIP seat in the arena. The boys were all coming to town.

I remember going to their suite and being surprised by the sight—strippers and guys passed out everywhere, condoms and empty bottles scattered across the room. The girls always broke the rules for the stars. But that wasn't Shaun. It wasn't his suite, and he wasn't part of that scene. Shaun carried himself differently: calm, reserved, with a sense of class. He wasn't the type to get drunk and sleep with prostitutes or leave a mess behind. He held himself to a higher standard.

Chapter Twelve

THE BOYS

ONE DAY, RICHARD TOOK ME TO HIS GOLF CLUBHOUSE. HE HAD told a bunch of guys that his "Cigar Guy" was coming to town. We got to the clubhouse and sat down at the bar. Guys started to gather, and there was anticipation. They wanted to be involved, and they wanted the show to begin. Richard knew a lot of the guys, if not all of them, and everything was cool.

It was all white guys with college degrees and big houses, all acting cool while wearing the strange golf clothes like checkered bell-bottoms, and sweaters tied around their shoulders. As I usually did, I found and cleared a table and started to unpack and display my cigars. Like always, this caused some commotion, as more and more guys appeared and the room was getting full. This wasn't a small room either; it was the bar and dining area of a prestigious private golf club in Chicago's northern suburbs.

While I unpacked my cigars, a guy came over to get a glance and saw a box of Bolivar Belicosos (torpedo or #2). He grabbed it and said, "These are mine!"

Another guy half a room away said, "Hey, put that down, and let the guy lay them out for all of us to see."

The guy with the box in his hand said, "I've been looking for these, and this is the one I want."

The second guy said, "Well, that's the same one I want, and you need to put it back."

The whole room went quiet. Everyone stared at these two guys and the show they were putting on. They were now raising their voices and moving toward each other, getting aggressive, and talking louder and louder.

The guy with the box really didn't want to put the box down. He tried to ignore the second guy. He turned to me and said, "How much? I'll just pay for these and be on my way."

The other guy said, "Hey, asshole, I told you to put the fucking box down and wait until he's ready and everyone gets a chance to see what he's got."

Now, a few more guys were getting involved, the adrenaline was increasing, and like puppies, all the guys were getting excited. It's bizarre how boys and men act, with the aggression and fighting. It all started in a flash and really over nothing. A room full of guys with good educations, money, and privilege were arguing over a box of cigars.

As it got heated, Richard calmly got up from his barstool and tried to defuse the situation. He towered over these two guys and put himself between them. He tried to just calm them down. It was so funny to me. You have two white adults with professional lives, and they are acting like high school boys, while the Black athlete is calmly trying to calm them down, which he could physically do in about ten seconds.

The guy with the box in his hand says to the second guy, "You're a crappy golfer!"

The second guy says, "I'm a better boxer than golfer," and it was on. They started to fight. They were on the floor and rolling around like kids, and I quickly started to pack my cigars into the bags. Richard started to help me, and the guys kept on fighting, and more guys got involved (I'm sure there was some alcohol involved). A few moments later, Richard and I were running across the green carrying all my bags. While they were fighting, it was becoming out of control, and I knew the cops would be there soon.

I told Richard we needed to get the hell out of Dodge before they got there. The cigars were illegal, and he's not supposed to be doing business in the golf club, plus he's a celebrity, and it would probably make the news. When I said that, he almost turned white and thought about it for a split second, and grabbed those heavy bags like they were pillows. Here we are running across the golf course like thieves. I first started running the way we came in, to the parking area where his car was, but he was running the other way.

He said, "We have to go this way. My house is this way!"

We ran our asses off, carrying all the bags and suitcases. We finally made it to his house; the garage was open, and we ran inside. We dropped off my bags and went inside to hide for a moment.

I met a few good guys through Richard who became friends and good cigar customers. Most of the time, nobody fought over them.

This was how my entire cigar customer base was built. I would meet someone through someone, and they would then introduce me to the next guy, and so on. All this time, cigars were getting more and more popular and expensive. I was selling fine, premium imported (smuggled) Cuban cigars. They weren't cheap. Most of the guys I was catering to were wealthy. Some were super wealthy; they had private jet planes, mansions, and everything.

I started going to Richard's house to hang out, and he took me around to people's places who wanted to see "The Cigar Guy." That's how I met 23.

23

I had been selling cigars to Shaun and Richard for a while, and I'd hung out with both of them together. I had asked Shaun if he could introduce me to 23, and he said it would be hard, since 23 was a super celebrity and not too open to the public. He said Richard was his boy, but that Richard respected 23's privacy to the max and wouldn't cross any lines either. The conversion ended with that, and I didn't push it. I wasn't really worried. My goal was to make money and build my gym and my life, not to meet athletes.

A few weeks later, Richard called me and asked me if I could get a certain box of cigars, a special edition box of Double Coronas, fifty cigars in an almost square cedar box. I had heard of it but hadn't ever looked or asked because they were expensive and exclusive. He said that 23 was looking for them. Now he got my attention, and 23 wanted a special box. Before this, 23 was getting most of his boxes of Cuban cigars from Canada, but Cuban cigars had become so popular that even the richest, most famous athletes couldn't get everything they wanted. I told him I would look.

On my next trip to Havana, I went to the Partigás factory store and looked for Abel, the manager. I had a good relationship with Abel, and I knew he could get me almost anything I wanted. When I got there, he was excited to see me and asked if I had a car. I did. My driver was outside with the car.

He gave me a ride and said, "We'll talk."

We got into the car and he began to tell the driver where to go. We talked about his brother, who he was trying to get out of Cuba. He told me he would like to get out too. I was still surprised to hear this, even though I knew what life was like in Cuba. He seemed to be set up, but even with his position and prestige, he wasn't living well at all. This is the kind of guy who gets a lot of attention from the international cigar world. He's in the magazines all the time. He's the kind of guy who gets invited to some cigar festival or business engagement for cigars somewhere in the world and defects and just doesn't return to Cuba ever again.

We didn't talk about cigars for the whole two hours we were driving around. We only talked about cigars when we were getting out of the car at Partigás. It was so nonchalant, and he said, "What are you looking for?" I said, "I need a special hard-to-get box." I told him, "It's for 23."

Abel could get the box for me. It was a special box, fifty of the finest hand-picked Double Coronas, a large square wooden box with fifty cigars wrapped with a yellow ribbon. The cigars were neatly arranged in a certain way so the entire bundle smoothly slid into the cedar wood box. This type of box uses a wooden top that slides in and out, not a hinged top.

I was so happy when I got the box. For some reason, it felt like more. I felt like it was some sort of accomplishment. I got something that few people could get. I was literally on the inside of the cigar world. Sure, there were some well-established companies and a few guys who knew a guy, but I was "boots on the ground" in Havana.

Once back in the USA, I got the box to Richard as fast as I could. I had specially wrapped the box like never before. I was also uneasy the whole trip. I was worried about this box for 23. Richard paid me $1,500 for the box, and even he was happy. Richard was as happy as I was when I got the box. I even asked Shaun why Richard was so giddy when I handed him the box. He said Richard was still starstruck by 23.

It wasn't long after that when I met 23, and I became his Cuban cigar supplier.

I was pretty excited that I was now selling cigars to 23. He paid cash and didn't play games with paying. He didn't ask for discounts either. I was told not to bother him with asking for signed stuff. I completely understood. When my friends found out I was selling cigars to 23, they, too, started asking if they could meet him and if I could have some stuff signed. It bothered me when they asked me, because I could only imagine how tired he was of that.

I'll always remember my times of being around the great boxing champ Julio Cesar Chavez, and how he was bothered everywhere he went, and I always thought that this could drive a man to drink or use drugs. I thought I would eventually get some really cool stuff signed by 23. I was thinking unusual stuff, baseball stuff (he had recently been playing baseball)—bat, ball, or glove—that would all be unique. Or maybe his golf balls or golf club. Everyone had basketballs and Bulls jerseys signed, but who has those other items?

What I do have is a large picture of 23 celebrating after his last championship win, smoking one of the Hoyo of Monterrey Double Coronas that I sold him the day before.

KINGS AND DIGNITARIES

When 23 asked me what kind of unique cigar I could get him, I told him I would ask around in Havana. I asked Jorge at the Marina Hemingway store, and he told me to talk to Andrea, who made the hand-rolled cigars there at the store and who had also been a trusted hand roller for Fidel Castro's personal cigars.

I had her make two special *masos* (bundles) for 23. She made an extra-large Belicoso or torpedo and an extra-large Salomon. They were absolutely beautiful and really special. They were made to perfection. She made them by hand, without a mold, and she used her special technique of newspaper to form them and substitute for a mold. I had to wait extra days in Havana for these cigars to be finished. They weren't fast to make, and they weren't cheap. These cigars were literally for kings and dignitaries.

I was so proud of these cigars. They didn't exist in any stores or magazines. They were truly unique, and I could obtain them. I took four bundles of these back with me, and 23 bought all four at $1,500 each.

When other guys heard of them, they all wanted them. As people started to learn that 23 had them, more and more people wanted them. I just couldn't get as many as I wanted. Andrea wasn't as motivated by money as you would think, and these were hard to produce. Jorge, too, wasn't going to allow her to work only for me. She did her day's work and went home. He needed her there, producing and appeasing as many clients as she could and not just catering to me.

I was proud of my accomplishment in getting these special cigars for 23, and he, too, was very happy. He called me to ask if I could get him another special box, Partigás Series 898. They were in an odd-shaped wooden and varnished box, and they weren't common or easy to get. Again, I got them too.

A few days later, I was at a friend's house, and my beeper was going crazy. Richard Dent was trying to find me. I called him. He was upset, and I could hear the stress in his voice.

He told me I needed to talk to 23, that he was upset and believed I was selling him fake cigars. *What?* I'd said I'd get him the best and most unique cigars that I could. I busted my ass to get him what he wanted and more. I called 23, and he said that "someone" told him these cigars were fakes. First, they don't have a band or ring on them, and second, they don't show up in any of the bullshit magazines or books! Here I was again, defending myself because some idiot had decided to give his opinion.

The guy broke out some cigar books, and they couldn't find them. Two seconds later, 23 was on the phone, asking me, "Yo, what's up with these cigars?"

Here I was in a small kitchen of friends of mine, almost hiding in the corner and speaking to a sports legend about some bullshit that was caused by a guy who doesn't know shit about what he's saying.

I assured 23 that they were not only the real deal but that they were the best and most unique in the world. I said, "Mike, these are for presidents and dignitaries. These aren't for peasants. These were handmade for you by the best roller in the entire island of Cuba." I was on the phone for ten minutes with him, trying to calm him down and reassure him that he wasn't cheated.

The next time I went to Havana, I had Andrea make a video for 23. At first, she wouldn't do it. She was shy. I pleaded with her, and Jorge, her boss, pleaded with her, but she was scared. I'm not sure what scared her the most, but she was scared, maybe scared of any kind of trouble she might have from the government.

After two days, I eventually convinced her to make the video. She said, "Hi, 23, these cigars are made for you."

I filmed her making more and showed some of the process. When I showed the video to him, he smiled and started talking about going to Cuba. Soon, I had both him and Shaun asking about traveling to Cuba.

I remember the first time I went to his house. I pulled up in my cigar car, a real beater. He had these huge metal gates with the number 23 in the center. His property was like a park with a long winding driveway, and the house was beyond large. As I pulled in, I saw 23 in the distance using his putting green. He was relaxing and golfing, even though he was supposed to be sick. It was playoff time, and he had missed a game or two because he was sick, but here he was looking strong and fresh. I immediately had suspicions. He didn't look sick at all, and he didn't play the last game, and his team lost. But was he really sick, or did they pull him so his team could lose and have an excuse so the series could go the distance? I still wonder, to this day, if pro sports are rigged. Maybe.

He greeted me and directed me over to his garage and told me where to park. We chatted for a few moments before he directed me into the house. As always, I opened the trunk and unloaded many bags full of boxes of Cuban cigars. Inside his kitchen, I opened the bags and laid out as much as I thought was needed. I knew he would only want the best and hardest to find, and maybe a few others as gifts for friends and others. He separated the boxes and asked questions about specialty boxes, and ordered a few boxes for the future. I asked if he was feeling better, and he looked up from where he was focused and said, "It's time to win." I didn't ask him to sign anything and didn't waste his time. He paid me, and I promptly left. Since that day, he has called me all the time, and even his wife called and would ask me, "Where is 23's favorite friend?"

I have an enlarged framed picture of him celebrating the next day when they won the championship. He has one of the cigars I sold him in his mouth.

Every time I look at the picture, it makes me think, what an amazing period of time. I was meeting great role models, learning, and making money. How many people have been so fortunate as I? I got the opportunities, and I rode the wave.

CLIMBING THE FOOD CHAIN

Now that I was buying 95 percent of my cigars in the factory stores and I was getting the *masos* from Papito, I had a new confidence. I finally felt good and safe about my product; I knew they were the same as what anyone could get from the Canadian cigar shops and European cigar shops. Since almost all my cigar customers were wealthy, many traveled around the world and had contacts or connections to get them from these places. One of my customers even had his own private locker at the Davidoff store in London. He had purchased a few very expensive boxes of pre-Castro cigars from them and would always bring back a few boxes when he came back to the States. Mine were cheaper, I had variety, and I brought them to their front door, literally. I was at their beck and call. I would go almost anywhere, anytime to service my customers.

I had one guy in particular who was on my mind. He was a young Greek guy, a bookie who had a lot of money and knew a lot of people. He could have been a great connection. Demitri was introduced to me by one of my customers, but he was not convinced of the legitimacy of my cigars from the beginning. As it was with most cocky guys, they think they know everything and automatically voice their opinion. It always got to me that they called them fakes. My cigars weren't fakes; they were all from Cuba.

My business was hurt from the beginning when my boxes arrived dinged and scuffed. It was amazing, but more people care about the image than the product itself. I get it, but it's still stupid. My cigars were 100 percent Cuban, and boy, oh boy, did I suffer to get them to their front door. I wanted so badly to win him over and get him to buy and stop talking badly about me. He knew a lot of people and would tell anyone who asked him that my cigars were fake.

When I sold mostly factory-bought cigars, I made another appointment with him. I went to an office he had in a strip mall, on the second floor of a main avenue in Chicago. I brought only the best boxes with me, and I prepared a "special bag" of the best and hardest to get.

It was early evening in the fall, and it was already dark. I went upstairs and was buzzed in, and led to a back office through a maze of cubicles, where there were girls taking bets.

He asked, "Why are you so persistent with me?"

I told him I wanted the opportunity to prove to him that my cigars were legit, because he was giving me a bad rep. If not for me dealing with businessmen and straight shooters, I would have given him a fucking beating for opening his mouth, but I didn't want that word getting around either. These guys definitely don't want to deal with a thug. It was a real test of my patience.

He was a young, good-looking guy, clean-cut, and very well groomed; his hair was perfectly groomed, nails too. He had a dark green Riviera that was immaculate, and he took care of himself and everything else too.

He barely even looked at the boxes I laid out on the table. From his front shirt pocket, he pulled out a small cigar box and showed me "his" cigars. He told me he had a supplier in Miami who sent him anything he wanted. The Miami cigars were notorious for being fakes! I couldn't tell him this, or I didn't even want to waste my time. He cared only about image. I eventually left there without a sale and without clearing the air.

That day, I learned it's all bullshit. His cigars were fake. But it didn't matter. He wanted those boxes, labels, and the image, and that was it. He smoked those Honduran-made cigars and felt like Al Capone. We left the building together and each got into our cars. He then called me over to his car, opened his glovebox, and showed me a package he had recently received from his contact in Miami (almost three times the cost of mine). I could see they were fakes from a mile away. But the box was pristine and flawless. His car was the same, and so were his clothes and his watch.

This guy was all about image, and nothing I did or said would change his mind. I gave him a box of five Montecristo No. 4s for free and told him to enjoy them, and we went our separate ways.

I got back into my car and sat for a moment. I was feeling down.

My car was a $1,000 piece of shit, old, beat-up, and ugly; my clothes were old and the same. Even the bags I carried were old and shitty. I just felt down.

I was just realizing my place in the food chain. There are so many people out there in the world with real lives. Yeah, I had made some money, I had a lot of wild adventures, but I never had a real life. I had lived on the fringes of society.

It's not like I hadn't been exposed to this level of people, but it was different now. I was in my early thirties, and I could now see the difference, or maybe I now had my eyes opened. I was building my customer book all the time. With every trip, I had more and more, and most of them were rich.

I had bar owners, owners of car dealerships, high-level lawyers, judges, restaurant owners, politicians, trucking company owners, professional athletes, radio personalities, the owner of the largest taxi cab company, jewelers, bankers, cigar store owners and employees, car salesmen, doctors, dentists, a renowned photographer, nightclub owners and managers, real estate developers, a limo company owner, McDonald's owner, health club owner, stockbrokers, bond traders, sports managers, you name it. The list goes on and on. I didn't have too many average guys as customers.

What I noticed was that none of them were so smart that they shone; some weren't even what I would consider smart.

I started to realize that I was smart. Hell, I was smarter than almost all of them. How did they make it to where they were? I started seriously asking myself that question. One of them was a billionaire. He had two private jets; he had paid $8 million to have the interior of his plane remodeled. Can you imagine that? Eight million dollars on new fucking seats! To this day, I'm still blown away; so much money just to sit and feel better about yourself.

It was like I was going through a master's course in life and finance. I would listen, watch, and learn. I was just as smart as any of them. None of them seemed to be superhuman, as I had expected people at that level to be. There were a few who were actually stupid—

very wealthy, but not very smart. Making money and keeping it is more about being consistent and pushing forward than about being smart.

I realized I really wanted more than I would ever get from the cigar business.

TRINIDAD CIGARS AND THE MYTH OF CUBA

Later on, when I was more established in my cigar business, a rumor went around that there was a secret brand of cigars, the Trinidad, so secret that no one had ever even seen them. Supposedly, it was a very special brand that was made exclusively for Fidel Castro. Fidel would give them to diplomats and VIPs he associated with. The myth was growing like wildfire, and I was getting asked all the time whether I could get Trinidads.

I told my customers over and over that it was a myth and not true, yet they continued to feed the flame, and it just grew. I was questioned and scrutinized because I couldn't get them. Some people were doubting my legitimacy because I couldn't get them.

I had already asked so many people in Cuba about them, even the director of the Partigás factory, Ernesto. It was always the same: a smile and a laugh. They didn't exist.

One day, I was walking down the street near my hotel in Vedado; the street ran parallel to the Malecón (boardwalk) that faced the ocean. It was the street behind the Riviera hotel. It wasn't a well-kept area, and the houses and apartments were falling down. This area hadn't seen a coat of paint in forty years. I was approached by two young Black guys offering cigars. Since this happened all the time, it was just normal. For some reason (their persistence), I agreed and followed them through a maze of walkways, hallways, and alleys into a small, dark, ground-floor living space. The place had very little natural light and smelled of humidity. An old Black woman was sitting on the doorstep with some sort of sickness. Her calves or lower legs were swollen, huge, and so strange-looking to me. I had never seen anything like it and couldn't help noticing. I thought it was the elephant disease, but what do I know, I'm not a doctor.

The guys started showing me their cigars. I first saw an obvious fake box of Cohiba Espléndidos; it was a glass-fronted box. I had seen these before and knew they were fakes. But they looked good. The glass front was a good idea from whoever invented them, but they weren't from the factory and were tagged as fake by anyone who knew.

Then out of the dark came a beautiful box with a piano-black finish. Trinidad! I was stunned for a moment. The box was nice, and the cigars had a gold band with black printing. They were slightly raised letters, beautiful lines, and so on. Now they had my attention. I wanted it. I needed it. But it was too expensive. The guy wanted $2,000 for it. Instead, I took a mental picture of it and paid attention to all the details.

The light bulbs were going off in my head; I had a rush of energy and a flood of ideas. I would do it even better. I would give my customers exactly what they wanted.

I went to Old Havana, where they had the street vendors selling books and antiques, and I found what I was looking for: Fidel's signature. I found it in an old book. Remember, there was no internet, and I didn't have easy options to find it, but there it was, right there in the book.

I bought the book and was on my way with a new plan: I would produce the exclusive brand that so many people were making me crazy over.

As soon as I was home in Mexico, I immediately started to develop the Trinidad brand. I first had to develop the size of the box; I needed it to be perfect. It had to fit twenty-five Double Corona cigars and have a wooden spacer on the bottom row; the bottom row of a cigar box had twelve cigars, and the top row had thirteen, total of twenty-five. They must fit perfectly and look pristine. They would be high-quality, premium cigars. Once I had the interior size perfected, I was ready to design the entire box, and it had to be beautiful.

The boxes were made out of the highest quality cedar wood I

could find; it had a reddish tone. The outside was glossy black with the three edges of the top slightly rounded, shiny, with gold-colored hinges in the back, which made it look elegant. I had to have three special punches made to indent the wood with the final touches. First, I had the name TRINIDAD stamped or embossed into the center of the top. Then I had another made with the signature of Fidel, which was placed in the lower-right corner. Both of these were then painted with gold paint, which made the boxes look amazing. Last, I had to stamp the official Habanos seal in the center of the bottom.

When I finished the boxes, they looked amazing. I had William help me design and print a Trinidad band, and once that was placed on the cigars and they were assembled into the box, it looked 100 percent legit.

The truth is, I never felt comfortable selling these to anyone, especially since most of my customers had become friends and were all good guys. I felt bad, and to this day it still bothers me. I didn't do it out of greed; I did it out of survival. With all the pressure, my reputation and my bottom line could have been affected if I didn't.

I must have made about one hundred boxes and sold them for $1,200 to $1,500 per box.

I didn't just show up with a bunch of boxes one day either. First, I couldn't have them made so fast. It took time to make them, and second, I needed to build up the emotions and prep the people for what was coming.

I started mentioning them, I "planted the seed," and they took care of the rest. I would say I had a contact in the government who was helping me track them down, etc. Slowly, I told or "leaked" the story, and soon my customers were asking me for them. I would only bring a few boxes with me. Sometimes, certain guys wanted to see them but couldn't because they had already been sold, and this would cause an increase in demand.

Fortunately for me, it was toward the end of my cigar smuggling days, and I didn't have to fend off so much negativity, although I was called out by a few people.

The funny thing is that Cuba did the same thing. Eventually, the Cuban powers that be learned about the international myth and started to produce the Trinidad cigar for the public. It was so much simpler than the ones I produced, and it was a Lancero size, long and thin, which is the same size that Fidel smoked, when he did smoke, before he quit. It's so funny, really; even the small, poor, and isolated island of Cuba figured out how to use marketing to its advantage.

Even though the Trinidad cigar didn't exist, they decided to go along with the charade.

Chapter Thirteen

GOOD FELLA

I MET A LOT OF PEOPLE IN CUBA: TOURISTS, HUSTLERS, TRAVelers from all over the world, but there's one guy I still remember to this day.

The moment he opened his mouth, I clocked the East Coast accent, probably New York. But when I asked where he was from, he said somewhere out West. *Bullshit*, I thought immediately.

He asked where I was from. "Chicago," I told him.

He nodded and said, "I know some people from there."

Okay.

He had a certain way about him—a little low-class swagger, rough around the edges but smooth enough to slide into any conversation. I noticed how much he smoked. He chain-smoked cigarettes one after the other. He even smoked cigars and cigarettes, sometimes back to back.

He wasn't big. Not fit. But he had an attitude. He carried himself like he knew something you didn't. He was a little cocky, a little slick. We talked for a while and swapped stories, but red flags just kept appearing. Something wasn't adding up.

Who was this guy?

It was right there, the name on the tip of my tongue, but I couldn't quite grab it. I kept studying him from different angles, catching him in different light, trying to put it together.

And then it hit me.

Henry Hill.

The infamous mob rat. The guy from *Goodfellas*. The one who flipped, disappeared, and ended up in witness protection, hunted ever since.

I kept staring, asking myself over and over, was it him?

I didn't want to be rude. I didn't want to spook him. I didn't want to push too hard and blow up his spot, if it even was him. But it drove me nuts that whole day.

Was it really Henry Hill?

FIDEL

As I evolved into an experienced cigar smuggler and salesman, I also learned more and more about Cuba and Havana.

Once, when we were staying in a nice apartment on Fifth Avenue, I woke up and went out for a run. I usually ran down the center of the avenue because it was wide and had a nice path in the center with benches and statues alongside. This was the upscale area of Havana, if there was one. Even though the streets went through the avenue, traffic was only allowed to cross at the stoplights; you couldn't cross at any street you wanted. There was also a police booth every two or three blocks, so the area was heavily guarded and secure. It was the area with a lot of foreign embassies and foreign business offices.

As I ran along the road returning to the apartment where we were staying, I noticed something was wrong. Different. I was feeling something. I couldn't tell you exactly what it was, but I felt something was off. I noticed that each of the stoplights was on red, there were cars backing up at each one, and as I moved from street to street, it was the same. The cops were out of their booths, and there were more than usual. I could feel something.

I could feel the change. I didn't know it in the moment. It took a few seconds to catch my bearings, but I could feel something. First, everything was normal...the cars and traffic, and then everything became almost like slow motion. There was a strange calm. No more cars, no more traffic, like time stopped. They were controlling the traffic lights and had made all the cross streets red, for a long distance, longer than I could see for sure. This gave Fifth Avenue all green lights with only one car moving (or three cars).

All of a sudden, I saw a three-car caravan, three Mercedes sedans, all three were exactly the same. They all had guys with submachine guns, all the guys had the same style beard, and the same style clothes.

And then I saw him. It was Fidel Castro. This was his motorcade. The bodyguards all looked like him, and they were all positioned at a window and almost hanging out of the window.

I could swear that I looked directly at him, Fidel Castro. It felt surreal. I was in another dimension for a brief moment. Time felt like it was in slow motion. It was just all slow until it was all over, and everything went back to normal.

Cuba was like that: the myth of Fidel and the hard-nosed business sense to market the Trinidads, and the poverty, and the girls, and all the people scrambling and selling anything they could to make a living. I always missed the modern world when I was there. Once, after a three-week stay in Havana, I literally kissed the ground once I landed back in Mexico.

When I really got started moving cigars, though, all that faded into the background, because smuggling cigars wasn't ever easy money. Anybody who thinks there's such a thing as easy money doesn't know what they're talking about. It took hard work, ingenuity, constantly solving new problems, and running into one barrier after another.

UPS SCARE

My life revolved around cigars.

I traveled to Cuba as often as necessary. Sometimes I'd stay for weeks if the factory stores were dry. If I had to wait, I waited. I had no choice. Meanwhile, back in Mexico, I was building out the new gym addition. Between construction, Cuba runs, border trips, and Chicago drops, every day was booked. My world was in motion all the time.

The border runs never followed a script. Sometimes the sales came easily. Other times, I had to force it: push hard, shake trees, hustle every deal. Chicago could take days or weeks. Nothing was guaranteed.

Because I was always moving, I leaned on different people to help at different times. This trip was no different. I left Guadalajara with my friend Tono. We took the bus north to the border. There, I ran through my routine of repacking cigars and prepping everything for the cross.

Ever since I lost that shipment in the river, I'd changed my method. I started sealing the cigar boxes inside clear plastic bags before wrapping them with stretch film. That inner bag provided a waterproof barrier. The roll sealed it all in. It wasn't perfect, but it gave me an edge.

I made sure Ramiro had everything ready for the crossing. Then I crossed to the US side, checked into my usual cheap motel, and waited. Once I got the product, I repacked it, boxed it up, and shipped it via UPS to my mother's house in Chicago.

Tono and I made our way to Houston by bus, then flew to Chicago. Once we landed, it was all about waiting. I never contacted clients ahead of time. That was by design. No one needed to know my schedule. And I refused to make promises until the cigars were in my hands. If I lost a shipment and couldn't deliver, I'd lose face. Simple as that.

But once I had them? It was game time.

I always called Gary Kron first. He was like an older brother: loyal, steady, and always first in line. Then I'd start working the list.

But this time, something felt off. A few days passed. No delivery.

I tried calling UPS to check the tracking. Nothing helpful. Just vague updates and bad hold music. I paced. Waited. Five days passed. Then six. Then seven.

Still nothing. I was starting to spiral. My gut said the load was gone. Another hit. Two steps back.

Then the phone rang.

A deep male voice on the other end said, "Scott? This is UPS. Your boxes are here, but...there was some damage. You'll need to come to the facility to retrieve them."

Immediately, my senses flared. Something wasn't right.

Everything in me said: RUN.

I grabbed Antonio. We jumped into my newly bought dark blue Chrysler minivan and headed to the UPS facility. The place was massive: a sea of warehouses, loading docks, and trucks, stretching across several city blocks.

We went to the main office. They looked at me blankly. No one knew about the call.

Red flag.

Tono could see it on my face. I didn't like this. The cigars were ten days late. Normally, they arrived in four. My nerves were shot.

Then someone came out and told me to drive to another building on the lot. "A guy's waiting for you," they said.

We got in the van and rolled slowly across the property. I scanned every face, every parked car, looking for anything out of place. Cops? Feds? Anyone watching?

We pulled up to the designated building. A large overhead roll-up door started rising. Inside stood three men. All in suits.

Fuck.

I didn't like the look of them. Not sharp suits. These were off-the-rack, federal-issue types. I'd seen that look before. I was staring at law enforcement. No doubt in my mind.

One of them walked over.

"Your boxes are inside, including the damaged ones," he said. "They're on pallets. Just pull in."

I looked at Antonio. He leaned close and whispered, "Don't go in."

My gut agreed. It smelled like a setup. Like I was already caught.

Still, I rolled forward...then pulled a hard U-turn. I circled the lot once, twice. I didn't know what the fuck I was doing. I just kept moving, trying to think. The three suits stood there watching me, probably thinking I'd lost my mind.

One of them waved me in again.

I played dumb. "Where? In there?"

He nodded. I stared him down for a second. Then thought, *Fuck it.* I drove into the warehouse. The door rumbled shut behind me. It was done.

I told myself: *Whatever happens, happens. I need my cigars. If I'm getting popped, then so be it.*

I followed the three men at a slow roll. One led us into another part of the warehouse through a wide entry into a new building. A wall blocked my view. I couldn't see what was coming next.

My heart pounded. I was fully in flight mode. I considered turning, bolting for the door. But I didn't. I followed them in.

I turned the corner. There they were: several pallets of boxes. Smashed, ripped, half-open—cigar boxes spilling out.

I froze.

I waited for agents to flood in, guns drawn, shouting for us to get on the ground. But...nothing.

Tono and I got out. The three suits barely even looked at us. They were off to the side, chatting among themselves.

I couldn't believe it.

We started loading the boxes into the van. I was still waiting for the trap to spring. Still watching the exits. But no one came. No questions. No search. Just an apology for the damage and a nod to the exit. We drove out.

Even then, I stayed sharp, scanning the mirrors, checking our tail. I expected unmarked cars to close in. But nothing happened. After a few blocks, the paranoia finally started to fade.

And then...I laughed. That wild, cracked laugh that only comes after you survive something real. My body flooded with adrenaline. It felt like freedom, like I'd just run a gauntlet and made it out the other side.

But it left me thinking. *What the hell am I doing to make a buck? Was this the trip that was supposed to end it? Could I stop now—if I had to?*

The answer was no.

I still had too much construction left. The new gym wasn't finished. The money I had wasn't enough. I had customers, momentum, and a name that meant something. I wasn't under the radar anymore. I was part of the game.

This wasn't the time to quit.

I still had work to do.

BIG DREAMS

My client list was growing steadily. I was at a point where I didn't really need any more customers, and I didn't have to win over every one of them. I was now a very seasoned person in the cigar medium, and I knew a lot more than anyone I had met so far. It was a nice sweet spot to be in. I had Ramiro at the border to cross my cigars smoothly, I had the method of shipping them to his brother's house, and I no longer had to travel with them. I also had a lot of contacts in Cuba and was getting almost any cigars I needed, on one trip or another.

My weeks were full. Even if I didn't have appointments or even sales lined up, I would make it happen. I had a business card holder. It was like a wallet, but it had pages and spaces for each card, and it was double-sided, too, so you could take advantage of both sides. I had all of my contacts' cards or their numbers written on paper and put into the booklet. I would sit down and stare at the contacts. I would think of reasons to call someone, anyone. I would leave messages at their offices with their receptionists. If they sent me a beep, that meant they wanted something. I would call everyone and anyone. It would always get things moving.

So, usually Monday through Friday, I drove from one side of the Chicago area to the other. I would try to consolidate and organize the same side of town around the same day and times, but it didn't always work out that way.

Saturdays were usually the day I drove around from bank to bank. I would cash checks and cash out. Over the week, I would accumulate a lot of checks. I would always ask them to make it out to cash, so there was no paper trail. It was like it never really existed. I would just turn the check into cash. Usually, the banks were all over the place and only open half a day on Saturday, so I would start early to get it all done. Sometimes I had customers to see on Saturdays and Sundays, but cashing the checks was a priority. I needed to make sure there was money in the account and prepare for my way out of town. I couldn't leave everything for the last moment.

So I would end up with a lot of cash everywhere on Saturdays: pockets, socks, jacket pockets. Saturday was like payday. I would also need to get back to home base to drop it off. I never wanted to be driving around with much cash, especially if I had cigars with me and was going to see customers. Because then if I got stopped or caught, I would lose my product and my money.

Once I had cashed all the checks and had my money straight, I would then evaluate what cigars I had left. If there were any customers, I could either sell some of the remaining boxes to them or leave them with someone who would pay me later. I was usually tired at this point and willing to break my own rules or even dump the product I had left at discounted prices. I had usually been in Chicago for a week or two, working long days and nights. It was strange. It almost always turned into a problem whenever I left cigars with someone without payment. It was like drugs. If they owed money for credit, they usually didn't want to pay later.

This whole time, when I was traveling back and forth between these three countries, I was also running my gym, and I was the general contractor for the project. I was also the person who had to pay for everything. It was a trying time in my life. The money was rolling in at a nice pace. I figured out how to save just enough to make sure I could pay emergency bribes if needed, and I believed that I needed enough cash on hand to buy two full loads if needed. I knew it would be terrible for business if I lost a load and didn't have the cash to get going again.

Anyone who has ever built something should know the dilemmas and struggles involved in construction. Almost all the people involved are basically thieves. There's no set price for everyone. They stick it to you the best they can, case by case, and then they make up the quote. Most of the building was brick, rebar, cement, and sand. We had to build the structure and the foundation first. This costs a lot, and you really don't see the progress. It's mostly buried and not visible. Then it was the columns, beams, and floors.

At the same time, we were using special engineers for the weight calculations, the soil preparation, and to align all the previous buildings together as one. It was a major project. The land was six thousand square feet alone, and we built two levels, plus the entire roof was covered with a thirty-foot-tall steel structure and covered with a metal roof; the sides were covered with a chain-link fence. This was a full basketball court and a fast soccer court.

To me, this was a major project and expensive. I was putting a lot of cash into the project every day. I knew in my heart that what I was doing was right. It was still hard, but I knew this would one day be the beginning of something big for me. I just stayed on course and kept grinding.

The entire building was built without a permit. I'm just not the kind of person to wait around for others to get moving, and I don't really like to stand in line. So fuck it, I did it without permits. At one point, I almost got shut down, but I became friends with the city inspector, Aldo, and for a fee, he became my permit. He made sure I didn't have to deal with bullshit. It wasn't for a few more years until that came back to bite me in the ass. I had a brand-new city inspector move in close to the gym, and a neighbor mentioned that the gym was built without permits, but that I had paid it off.

The new gung-ho inspector opened a can of worms that took me several years and $50,000 in fines to get everything straightened out.

I usually returned from the USA with $70,000 in cash. I had two Cuban girls with USA visas who would strap it to their bodies and still wear tight, provocative clothing. It didn't cost me much, and it was convenient. I also did it myself a few times. Money laundering wasn't even common back then, so it was less sophisticated. Even considering this, it still would have been a big clusterfuck to get detected with that amount of money in any part of the world. That $70,000 was approximately the money from 200 boxes at $350 a box. I would immediately take $15,000 and use it for the next few trips to Cuba to buy more cigars and then spend the rest on construction costs. It would go fast, and I was more often than not pressured because of bills and expenses.

This whole time, I had a family at home, two small girls in private schools with a few salaries of helpers at home, food, bills, etc. Life isn't cheap.

I often dreamed about my future life. I would be the owner of a nice-sized health club; it wasn't going to be a gym anymore. I would end up buying five total properties, all connected and joined into one, built into four stories and 40,000 square feet. Semi-Olympic swimming pool, two racquetball courts, weight room, boxing area with a full-size ring and many punching bags, a fifty-foot-tall indoor climbing wall, and a basketball court.

Over time, I was seeing all of my hard work accumulate; I could see it, and I could feel it. This motivated me even more. So I pushed forward with tunnel vision; against all odds, and with complete knowledge of all the risk and danger, I stayed focused. There were times I was exhausted, and so many times when I needed money, more and more again, and I couldn't see it. Then I'd see my way forward again and keep going.

Chapter Fourteen

POOR ANDERSON

ANDERSON WAS MY BRAZILIAN FRIEND. I'D FIRST MET HIM through Jaime, my driver. From the start, they were both prying, trying to figure out how I was getting my cigars out of Cuba and all the way to the USA. But that was my most guarded secret. It was the biggest problem everyone faced, and I never shared my secret with anyone. Those were trade secrets, and leaking them could ruin my system overnight.

Anderson had a brutal time trying to get his cigars back to Brazil. Most flights home were routed through Miami, and that's where his nightmare began.

As a Brazilian citizen, he had no problem traveling to Cuba. That part was easy. But the cigar game was changing fast. US Customs had started searching planes and luggage coming out of Havana. Even if you were only in transit, if your bag had Cuban cigars, they were gone.

Anderson learned this the hard way. They seized his entire suitcase. He tried to talk his way out of it, but it didn't matter. Gone.

A few months later, it happened again, this time in Brazil. He'd lined up a friendly customs agent to clear him, but when he landed, the guy was nowhere in sight. Another full loss. And this time, they fined him on top of it.

Anderson was starting to crack. You could hear it in his voice. He knew if he could just get the cigars into Brazil, he could make real money and build his connections. It was a golden opportunity, but only for people willing to risk it all. Most would have quit. Curled up and cried. But not Anderson. He kept pushing.

By this point, he'd taken two major hits, had a couple of small wins in between, and when it all balanced out, he was probably just breaking even. But it was getting harder. The street cigar scene in Havana was tightening up. He was always on the hunt for a new contact he could bribe at the airport, someone who could walk his boxes through. But every month, more doors were closing.

Then came the crash.

Anderson got caught at the Havana airport with several hundred boxes of street cigars. They hit him with multiple charges, including bribery, and hauled him straight to jail.

When I arrived and heard the news, I was shocked. Jaime had already been working the streets for weeks, trying to get answers. He was like a spy, hanging around outside police stations, chatting up anyone who might know something. Piece by piece, he built the picture.

At first, he was optimistic. We'd never seen a foreigner actually serve serious time for cigar stuff. There were plenty of horror stories, but most were just rumors. Even my own run-ins with Cuban authorities hadn't been that bad.

But time dragged on. And Anderson stayed locked up.

Six months passed. Still nothing.

Finally, about nine months in, Jaime managed to get us in to see him.

He looked like a ghost. Broken. He was still wearing the same clothes from the day of his arrest—filthy, torn, and stinking. His hair was long, his beard wild, his body rail-thin. Hollow.

He cried when he saw us. Not just tears but full-on sobbing. He begged us to get him out. Pleaded like a child. That's when I knew the Anderson I'd known was gone.

He was finally released after more than a year. Escorted straight to the airport and deported. I never saw him again. He never came back to Cuba.

And I don't blame him.

That whole ordeal made me realize just how lucky I'd been. If I hadn't pivoted when I did and gotten away from street cigars and into factory supply, I could have been Anderson. I listened to my gut. And it probably saved me.

Things were getting worse, not just in Cuba, but everywhere. Customs crackdowns. Jail time. Broken dreams. The cigar world was saturated. Too many people were chasing quick money off passion and contraband.

I didn't worry about trouble in Cuba anymore. I was clean. I bought from government stores, paid full price, and kept all my receipts. Everyone knew me. On every trip, I filled at least one suitcase at the airport shop. Under the circumstances, I was about as legit as you could be.

I flew in regularly, sometimes alone, sometimes with others, and I'd spend real money and keep to a pattern. When I ran into old contacts from the street game, I made sure they knew I didn't touch street cigars anymore. If they were informants, and some surely were, they could confirm I was playing it straight.

But the real problems for me started once I left Cuba.

Mexico was a minefield. And the US? They were catching on too. Customs agents were sick of the cigar craze. People were getting charged federally just for sneaking them in.

I might have been cleaner than most, but the game was shifting.

And Anderson…he was proof of what happened if you didn't evolve.

PLEASE, THANK YOU, EXCUSE ME: THREE PHRASES TO SURVIVE PRISON

None of the other cigar guys had what I had. They didn't speak Spanish, didn't travel, didn't have Cuban photos, Cuban stories, or Cuban scars. They didn't have a hot Latina wife by their side or real-deal street experience behind their pitch. They just sold cigars. I sold the lifestyle, and now I have the jars.

The ceramic Cuban cigar jars cost me twenty dollars each. They were overpriced, but I didn't have a direct source yet. Still, they looked beautiful. Retro, colorful, collectible. They came eight to a box, about fifty boxes total. I loaded every box into the Suburban and drove them north.

I crossed the load at Reynosa into McAllen, Texas. Ramiro helped with the cigars while I dealt with the import company and paid the fees. Once across, I prepped and shipped the cigars via UPS. Then I hit the road for Chicago, loaded down and running solo.

The drive through South Texas was tense. That stretch between the Valley and Houston is one of the most active drug routes in the country. Cops everywhere. Every few miles, someone was pulled over, cars torn apart, drugs pulled from trunks and fenders. I was rolling through in a bright blue Suburban with Mexican plates, overloaded with boxes. I looked like a damn target. Every time I saw flashing lights or a police cruiser creeping up, I braced for it, but somehow, I slid through.

By the time I got to Chicago, I was worn out but excited. The jars looked great. Customers liked them. They'd crack the tops, hear the pop, smell the inside. But they were fragile and heavy, and carrying them with all the cigar bags was a hassle. Still, I was making sales.

One of my customers gave me a tip: there was a new cigar shop out in the suburbs that I should hit. Big plans, big investor, former stockbroker turned cigar guy. I'd never been there before, but I got the owner's name and figured I'd drop in cold.

The place was impressive, I'll give him that. Once just a small tobacco store, he had transformed it into a cigar lounge complete with leather sofas, big TVs, a pool table, and dim lighting. He was going for a "Cuba meets country club" vibe. He said he wanted the biggest "Cuban humidor outside of Cuba."

I pulled up in my truck, my wife with me, jars in the back. We parked in the rear, walked in through the back door, and went straight to the counter. I asked for the owner. He didn't know I was coming, but he knew who I was. The cigar world is small, and I make noise wherever I go.

He came out of the back office and immediately zeroed in on her—hot Latina, tall, confident. He switched on. Eyes lit up. He invited us into his office like we were royalty.

And that's where it started—the performance.

He puffed himself up like a peacock. Bragged about his Corvette. Told me, in front of her, how he negotiated $5,000 off the sticker price. Went on and on about the dealership screwing up the delivery date, how he used that to leverage a better deal. He made me translate every detail for her. "Tell her," he kept saying. "Tell her how I did it."

She was confused. She didn't know why this guy was telling a car story. I knew exactly what was happening. This was his mating dance. His weird way of saying, "Look what I can provide if you were mine."

He didn't even try to hide it. Asked if she had a sister. Asked where she was from. Asked how we met. Then he kept using me like a translator-prop while trying to seduce her across the desk.

I tried to keep it focused on business. I brought in the jars. He liked them—a lot. Said he wanted them all. But then he started negotiating like a dick. Wanted them for ten dollars each. I told him they were eighty dollars, firm. I had $10,000 of my own money invested and wasn't going to walk away like some bust-out hustler just to unload weight.

But he pushed. Smug. Cheap. Obnoxious.

Then came the insults. He started talking about my clothes. Made little digs in front of her. Tried to clown me while making himself look like the alpha. He was trying to impress her by tearing me down. He was testing the wrong guy.

I could feel it—the shift. That tightening in my chest. The old street instincts waking up. I was trying to stay calm, trying to stay the businessman. But he kept pushing. He thought he was untouchable. Like a Howard Stern type—say anything, insult anyone, and walk away clean.

Except he wasn't Howard Stern. He wasn't anybody.

I stood there and stared at him. He made one more comment, something snide about my appearance, and I snapped.

I didn't punch him. I just slapped him. Open hand.

He dropped straight back into his leather chair, dazed. Out for a few seconds. My wife froze. She hadn't followed most of what was said in English, but the slap told her everything. I grabbed her hand, turned, and we walked out—clean. Truck. Parking lot. Gone in under thirty seconds.

Driving away, I explained the whole thing to her. She still didn't get why he told her a story about buying a car. I told her it was his weird way of trying to seduce her. He was flexing his wallet, his "power," trying to show that he could take care of her. But he did it by trying to humiliate me.

That doesn't fly where I come from. In my world, if you try to steal a man's woman in front of him, using disrespect as your weapon? You might catch a slap. Or worse. Don't be rude: please, thank you, and excuse me go a long way.

I thought there might be fallout. Calls from customers. Complaints. Gossip. But nothing ever came. Maybe he knew better. Maybe he was too embarrassed. Or maybe he realized, even in his ridiculous ego bubble, that he had crossed a line.

I never went back. Never needed to. I sold all the jars, piece by piece, for almost $100,000 total.

ON MY OWN

I hung around with Dick and Gary often. Gary liked to have me around for some reason. I know he liked and approved of me. His friendship with Dick was new. They had known each other, but the companionship grew since I brought them together through cigars. Dick was extremely wealthy, and Gary had some money and a few valuable properties, but Dick was very rich. It's not easy trying to keep up with someone else's lifestyle if it's too different from yours. Gary told me on a few occasions that he sometimes struggled to keep up with Dick's money.

I had been looking at a building on Main Street in Guadalajara. It would be perfect for a gym, I thought. It would also be perfect for an investment. It wasn't for sale, but it was abandoned. At this time in the late 1990s, money wasn't as free and easy as it became later. I found the owner, Mr. David Luna, and he set a meeting at his country/golf club. It was a very exclusive club in GDL. We met for a late lunch. He offered me the property for $250,000, and he would finance me for five years with a high interest rate, so high that in the five years with a balloon, I would end up paying double for the building: $500,000.

I wanted it badly. I was already planning the layout in my mind. I was already living it! If I'd bought it, I would have done well. The entire street and area have been gentrified, and the building is worth ten times what I would have paid.

I was excited to talk to Gary and Dick about my opportunity and plans. I was confident that if I consulted them, I would get some good advice. They were both millionaires, and Dick was on his way to becoming a billionaire. I had this romantic illusion that they would counsel me into a good deal. I thought it would be like a business meeting, and they would shoot options back and forth until we had a good plan.

That didn't happen. It was a Sunday morning, and we met at Gary's condo in the city, and as usual, I had all my bags of cigars. We were talking and socializing, and Dick was trying to convince Gary that he should buy his old house. Gary was explaining why it was too big a leap for him to take at the moment. Gary said the yearly property taxes alone were too much for him to want to pay; it was far from the city, and his business was too. I wanted to cut in and ask these two older businessmen how I should approach the owner of the building I wanted to buy, and how should I counter his financial offer? I had so many questions.

Here I am in a room with two well-established businessmen. I think they can coach me into making a good deal on the property, and since we're buddies, they'll be interested and passionate about it. As they were talking and looking over my cigar inventory, all I could think about was when would be the right time to start a conversation about my topic. I'm anxious. I can feel my body like it's going to explode. I want to interject and get talking about my issue, but I just don't feel the right opportunity to chime in.

These guys are going back and forth while smoking my cigars, and here I am just focused and waiting for the right moment. They both choose their boxes and make their personal stack of boxes that they want. I give them both their total, and they start to pull out money. Gary pays me. I count it and put it in my pocket while Dick is still fiddling around with his wallet. He needs to pay me $3,300. He has asked me twice already what he owes me. He gives me a stack of bills, and I start counting. I focus on the money and don't look up.

I finish counting it and pause, thinking I must have made a mistake. Only three thousand, so I count again. I still haven't looked up. I count again, and there's still $300 missing. Again, I pause, not sure if I made a mistake. I slowly look up and saw Dick smiling.

Here's a soon-to-be billionaire, and he's shorting me for three hundred bucks! He had watched me this whole time. I was struggling to understand what was going on, and he just watched.

I said, "Dick, three hundred dollars is missing."

He said, "Come on, give me a break. Take a few bucks off."

I was speechless for a moment, and then I saw the three hundred in his hand. He showed it and offered it, but when I reached, he pulled it back, smiled, and again asked for a discount. Everyone wants a deal, even a billionaire. He did finally give it to me, but it left me feeling strange.

Once all the business was finished, I was sure I would soon have my moment. The atmosphere was the same, just chitchat and socializing. I was now trying to force my issue, and I had almost shut out their conversation. I didn't want to miss this opportunity with two great business minds in the same place on a lazy morning with time to waste.

I almost got it out, but they just rolled on with their conversation. I was like someone waiting on the side to jump into the momentum. I was trying hard, and I blurted out a few times, but they didn't even pay attention, nothing. So I forced it. I stood up and cut in. I said, "Guys, I have a favor to ask." Now they both looked at me. They were still and quiet for a moment. I said, "Guys, I need your advice on buying a commercial building. I want you to help me come up with an owner finance deal that's good for me."

They didn't even give me one minute of attention. It was just seconds, and they were back to their conversation and paid no mind to what was so important to me.

I felt disappointed. I had waited a month for this moment, and it was a failure. I did learn and confirm that no one gives a shit about someone else's dreams. No one cares about anyone else. I was on my own and would have to face life alone. I had expected so much, and it was a great disappointment.

I didn't buy that building, but I wish I had. The neighborhood was all built up and redone a few years later. That building is now completely remodeled and worth twenty times what I would have paid for it in 1997.

Although I didn't buy that building, I opened a gym close to the same spot. It was a much better location, but I had to pay rent.

That was one of the moments that made me realize I was getting tired of being "the cigar guy." I wanted to build my own business. And now I knew no one was going to help me out. I had to do it on my own.

ASHTRAY JOHNNY

I met Johnny through the network. I sold him cigars from time to time, and occasionally he played middleman. Though like most middlemen, he didn't want to do much. Just point his finger and take the lion's share.

He lived in a modest house just outside the city. In the basement, he produced what he proudly called his world-famous cigar ashtrays. I'd drive over now and then to shoot the shit, and of course, he'd always mooch cigars. He bragged about the letters of appreciation he'd received. He had one from President Bill Clinton, framed and hanging on the wall. He gave me two of his high-end ashtrays once. I still have them. Now they're considered retro.

Believe it or not, there were a lot of cigar moochers. It drove me nuts. But Johnny was harmless. Just a regular guy trying to make his way. And life's not easy for a "regular" guy. I liked him. We weren't friends, but he was decent enough.

One day, he said, "Come on, Scotty, let me make a few bucks."

He knew I wasn't the kind of guy you could squeeze for freebies. But he was relentless.

We had talked plenty. He knew I was a street guy. He knew people I knew. I'm sure he'd heard stories. But men are stupid, and they do stupid things.

I finally caved and left him with about $10,000 worth of cigars. The deal was simple: he sells them, makes a little something for himself, and pays me back. If it worked, I'd front him more.

Why not? I'd done this for others. Let them make money while they move product for me.

I left town.

A week passed. No word. I called. No answer.

I waited another day. Still nothing. I started asking around, mainly to make sure he was okay before I got belligerent. People said he was fine. Then came the questions: "What's going on, Scott?"

"He owes me ten grand, and he's avoiding me."

"Oh yeah…he's not the best when it comes to paying."

"Oh, really?" I said. "Well, he'll pay me. That, I can guarantee."

I left him a voice mail:

"Hey, John. This is the guy you owe ten thousand dollars to. I'm not going to just disappear. You might feel safe now 'cause I'm far away, but let me remind you, I'm from Chicago. I'll be back, and I'll see you. I suggest you get your shit together."

He didn't respond. Now, I was careful. I wasn't about to leave anything on a recording that could get me arrested. And I wasn't playing with real guns anymore either. I was doing everything I could to walk a straighter line. I was a street guy in remission, trying to stay that way.

But this was a test.

When I got back into town five or six weeks later, I went to a sporting goods store and bought a BB gun. It looked exactly like the real thing. (I later sold it to my printer, William, because he liked it so much.)

Then I called Stu the Jew.

We pulled up to Johnny's place. Stu knew the drill. This wasn't our first ride like this. I walked to the side door and rang the bell, staying out of sight. As Johnny approached, I stepped into view.

He looked like he had seen a ghost.

I smiled to disarm him. He opened the door, and I grabbed him by the neck, shoved him backward into the kitchen, into the wall.

"You owe me money," I said. "And I told you: don't fuck me, John. But you did. You tried."

I had one hand gripping his throat and the other resting on the handle of the BB gun tucked in my waistband. He looked down and saw it.

"Johnny, don't make me pull it. Because if I pull it, I have to use it. Do you understand?"

He nodded.

"Now, do I need to tie you up and search the house? Or are you gonna pay me what you owe?"

"I'll pay! Let me get it," he stammered. "I was going to call you…"

"I'm sure you were," I said. "So we're both lucky I stopped by."

He turned to go downstairs.

"No," I said. "I'm going with you."

We went down to the basement, which was part workshop, part office, part factory. He paid me. I took the money, raced back up the stairs, and walked out to the car.

Less than five minutes, start to finish. Stu took one look at my face and knew it was handled.

And that was it. I never saw Johnny again.

CONSCIENCE OR CONTRABAND

Larry called from Mexico City. Fresh off a Havana trip, he'd somehow slipped a suitcase of cigars past customs. Now his big-shot "friends," the ones who swore they could get his stash into the US, weren't answering his calls. He was screwed.

"Where are you at?" he asked.

"GDL."

"I'm on my way."

That same day, he showed up at my apartment with one suitcase—about twenty-five boxes of the best factory originals money could buy. Larry always bought the top-shelf stuff. It wasn't about profit. It was about the image. Smuggling cigars got him into rooms and made him feel important.

We ran around Guadalajara for days while he tried to line up a crossing. He bragged about knowing all the right people, but nobody came through. Finally, he pinned his hopes on one last contact—Pepe Cohn in Juárez.

I knew Pepe. A cousin of my wife's family. Redheaded stepchild, literally. Not close, but connected. If anyone could make something happen, maybe it was him.

Larry left the suitcase with me. "Send it when I tell you where," he said.

A few days later, I got a drunken call. Larry had been physically tossed out of an Indian casino in New Mexico. Who knows what he did?

Up to then, I hadn't opened his case. But when he asked me to store the cigars in my humidor room, I unpacked every box carefully. All high-end brands. All my kind of product.

Then the delays started. False alarms. Wasted days. Every time I handled his cigars, the thought crept in a little deeper. Maybe I take a little slice for my trouble.

One box. Then another. Then all of them.

I'd repack his suitcase, then unpack it again, staring at the $25,000 sitting in front of me. I asked myself the same question I always did: *Will this guy ever be my friend?* No chance.

I didn't respect him. Out of shape. Drank too much. Gambled like a degenerate. Cocky. Spoiled rotten by his rich father. A useless man pretending to be a player.

So I burned him. Call it gangstering, call it bad habits. I took his shit.

Still, my conscience started buzzing. So I did what I thought was "fair." I bought cheap street cigars, packed his suitcase, and sent it by bus to Juárez.

I knew exactly when he'd open it. The phone rang seconds after the bus was due.

"I sent you the case as is," I told him. "Whatever happened to your boxes ain't my problem."

Later, he sent me a long letter, practically begging for them back. But I was done with him and with the business. When I'm done, I'm a ghost.

Yeah, I know, I sound like an asshole. But that day, I made $25,000 and balanced the scales on some of my losses.

Chapter Fifteen

THE WRITING IS ON THE WALL

I KNEW FROM THE BEGINNING MY CIGAR WORLD WAS TEMPOrary. Like every wave in my life, I rode it while it lasted and worked out. I was once told by my wise friend Tino, "Life sends us some waves and we must ride them while they last." He was a very wise man, and he just knew a lot of what most people didn't know.

There were signs all around me: People were now getting arrested in both Cuba and the US. It was always getting harder to get the cigars out of Cuba and into Mexico. Prison time had become a reality for people on both sides: Cuba and the United States. Jorge had left Cuba, and Abel wanted to leave too. The cigar craze was at its peak, and I knew it wouldn't be long before people turned their backs and started with the next fad. There was an organized group of Cubans out of Miami who were producing perfect copies on a large scale. They were hurting business.

Mario El Azabache had left the border and was living in LA. Oscar was a full-blown drug dealer in Chicago, and I mostly stayed away from him. He was bringing kilos of coke and a big weight of weed.

I got a call from Ramiro's brother, Lupe, asking if I had heard from him. He said it had been a week since anyone had seen him. He was deep into the underground in Reynosa. He didn't do anything else except transport drugs and other stuff across the border. He was a great contact for me, and he was always straight with me: no bullshit, no games. Once he disappeared, I was sad. I knew he was dead. The thought of starting all over and finding a new passage for my cigars was a dreadful thought. I had been doing it for almost four years, and I knew it was coming to an end. People can deal with certain difficulties for a period of time, but once the mind starts to reject them, it's almost over.

It's a funny thing: no one ever really knew anything else about me. All they knew was that I did my cigars. Sure, they knew, many people knew I was "selling" cigars, but that was it. They didn't know more. They didn't ask because no one cares. Really, no one gives a fuck about anyone else's struggles. I don't think anyone ever saw the inside of my humidor. No one ever helped me rotate boxes or wrap and prepare for a trip. I was very private about it. I did my thing and didn't tell. I also didn't want anyone to know I was making big money (it felt big to me).

Most people don't look at a guy selling Cuban cigars and say, "Hey, Pablo Escobar." This only happened once. Mark, the little fat Jew who managed the athletes and had the large ad agency, was smart (he kind of looked like George from *Seinfeld*). Mark looked at me and said, "Hey, you must be making a fortune," and he started adding it up, and he was fairly accurate. I was surprised and felt uncomfortable. I smiled and laughed. He said, "You're taking in a lot of money, and it's all cash."

Not only did he see it, but he was adding it up. He and one of his employees. Mark was lying back on his couch, and he started with the numbers. He said, "So, you bring three hundred boxes per trip, at an average of four hundred dollars per box. That's a hundred and twenty thousand dollars. Fuck, you make more than me! And this is all cash. You make cash."

I was surprised. This was the first guy who picked up on it. Once,

Gary Kron said something about me being well-spoken and having a good work ethic. Gary straight out asked me, "You have properties, right?" This was like from one Jew to another. I said yes, a few. At that time, I had my mother's house, a cabin with twenty-five acres in Wisconsin, and my existing gym with the expansions.

Since I dressed modestly and drove crap cars, they all assumed I was just their service provider. It was exactly what I wanted. But I was secretly striving to steal a life like the one most of them already had. I was working hard on all fronts. I guarded this personal secret like a starving thief who had just stolen a piece of bread. I wasn't going to let anything spoil my plans, and opening your mouth can destroy plans. I never told anyone my full name. I was known simply as "Scott Mexico."

Yeah, I had those moments where I felt less than them. They had the big expensive cars, and the great houses or apartments. Some had expensive jewelry and clothes, etc. I did feel the urge to want to fit in and shine, too, but I controlled it and resisted. *Stay the course, and keep your goal in sight.* I was making a higher life for myself the whole time.

Gary once invited me to a private, exclusive fundraiser for then–President Bill Clinton. I was pumped. This was my shot to meet the President of the United States. Gary handed me the paperwork, and a Secret Service contact to get my background cleared.

And that's when it hit me like a brick wall. When you've lived the life I lived, your past is never really gone. You can clean yourself up, run businesses, raise a family, and keep your name out of trouble, but being a felon is a brand you carry to the grave. It's the shadow that walks into the room before you do. It's the whisper you can't hear but know is there.

The thought of the Secret Service digging through my history, pulling up every arrest, every investigation, well, it was like a movie reel I'd seen too many times. I wasn't about to put myself under that microscope or risk my name floating through those circles. My guilty conscience got the best of me. I made up some excuse and walked away from what Gary would later call a once-in-a-lifetime opportunity.

He told me afterward that more than a few of my boxes had already made their way into Clinton's private humidor. He even had a photo of himself handing the president a box of Hoyo de Monterrey Double Coronas straight from my hands, through the pipeline, and into the White House.

It's a strange feeling knowing the President of the United States may have leaned back in the Oval Office, lit up one of my smuggled cigars, and enjoyed every pull, while the man who got it there couldn't even pass the clearance to shake his hand.

BUILDING A NEW GYM

Not long after I stopped selling cigars, and while running my finished gym for a while, I started looking into McDonald's and other franchises. I had mostly wanted to do White Castle hamburgers in Mexico. To me, they were the most similar to the street taco. The street tacos were available almost everywhere, and they were small and greasy. I thought the twenty-four-hour White Castle burgers would be a hit. Since I had known Johnny and had some insight into his world, I pursued McDonald's. I called them all the time and pursued it as hard as I could. They eventually sent me to the person in charge of the Mexican territory, and he was almost impossible to locate.

Then one day, I sat down to think about what I was doing. I had been involved in the gym/health club environment for a while now, and I had owned my own gym for close to ten years too. If I were to get further involved with my burger adventures, it would take a lot of time to understand and dominate the know-how of this new world. *Do I really want to invest the next five to ten years learning about a whole new business? What are the pros and cons?* I thought. At that time, an average Gold's Gym franchise made approximately $200,000 profit for the owner, and that alone made me decide that I was better suited to continue in my industry and just duplicate my footprint, which meant opening more gyms.

There was an old, abandoned grocery store on Main Street in GDL.

It had been abandoned and available for rent for years. The economy wasn't great, and the area was old and no longer popular. I drove past the place a few times a week, and one day I thought, *What if? What if I put a gym here?* I mentioned it to my wife, and she was neutral. I talked about it all the time and dreamed about it, but I was still traveling all the time for the cigars, and I didn't have the money to do it either.

I was driving from the border to Chicago alone and geeked out on coffee. My mind raced with this idea. I was planning, designing, and managing it in my mind already.

I even called home one time because I was thinking about this. I hadn't even finished the construction of my first gym, and the dream of this new one began. It was a strong pull. Something was telling me, "Do it." Pull the trigger and take the chance. I had someone get the number and ask how much the rent was. It had been vacant and abandoned for at least six years.

The neighborhood wasn't popping, and it was kind of a sleepy area. I did open the gym there; it took me nine months of arduous labor to tear out the old stuff and build out the gym. It looked spectacular once it was done. Not only did it look right; it was right. This place was rock and roll for a long time.

THE END AND THE BEGINNING

I had always known my whole life that whatever you're doing that's illegal or illicit will eventually come to an end and often violently; it can't last. There are too many forces against you. When I got involved with the cigars, I was conscious that this wasn't going to be a forever business. I knew it was a get in, make and save as much as you possibly can, and get out. A few years max. I had also programmed myself to take full advantage of the chance. It wasn't really illegal (not in my mind), but it could be if I got caught.

Once my gym construction was near the end, I knew it was time to get out. It had been a good run, and I had made enough money to build my gym. I had started hearing stories about people getting busted. They were actually starting to put people in prison for the cigars, and there was a serious federal charge they could apply if they wanted. Plus, there was an official embargo against Cuba.

I didn't tell anyone. I didn't say goodbye to anyone, not in Cuba or the USA. I guess I could have made a lot on one last run too. If I had told all my customers I was quitting and to stock up, I could have sold a thousand boxes for a higher price or whatever, but that wasn't what I wanted. I just turned off my beeper, put my contact folder into a drawer, and walked away. I did feel like a dick sometimes. These people had been a big part of my life for almost four years, but I knew if I told them, there would be some drama and bullshit I didn't want to deal with. I didn't need any long goodbyes.

I think I got everything I wanted out of it. I ended up with my gym, bigger than life for me. I would now focus on that new part of my life, running a real business, building a life, brick by brick. I would make a living while learning how to manage a life, save money, and make wise decisions with that money.

I want to get this straight: I made money through my Cuban cigars, but it was *never* easy. I didn't use Cuba or take advantage of anyone when they were down. I think I put back in what I took out. Yes, I had a few great romances. Yes, my friends laid down more pipe than ever in their lives up until the current day. Yes, we had loads of fun, but I was reciprocal. I helped Jorge escape. I paid everyone well and made sure to bring gifts and shop for specific items for people, and I never once asked to be paid back. I respected everyone and never looked down on anyone for their uncontrollable situations. I understood and empathized since the beginning. Once survival kicks in, we all would do the same.

When I started, I was looking for something, and as time went on, I got closer to what I was looking for. I had finished the gym construction and started thinking a lot about the equipment I would need. I didn't have much cash saved because almost all the money I could get was being reinvested into sand, dirt, cement, and everything else for the gym.

I would sit at my desk in an office I had built in the lobby area of the existing gym. At this point in my life, I was fine dealing with people and their bullshit all day long, so I had a clear glass office in view of everyone. I would sit there and work on the plans for the construction. I would think about colors, where to put stairs, walls, and windows. Everything. I was constantly thinking of ways to make the gym better.

I started looking for gym equipment locally. I knew a few people who had closed a gym and had some equipment put away in storage, but nothing good came out of those leads. I actually went against my better judgment and even consulted local manufacturers of gym equipment. I was planning and trying to make the amount of money that I thought I would have for equipment stretch and buy a full package. I was growing the gym by a significant amount of square footage, so I would need a full gym package. I needed more equipment than I could pay for. I had a local guy really pushing me to buy his equipment, and if he had been able to produce it faster, I probably would have made a huge mistake and bought it.

Luckily, my better judgment took over, and I didn't buy locally made equipment. I took a flight to LA. A few years earlier, I had met a guy, Craig, from CSM Fitness. He was the owner of a used gym equipment company, and he was the only one I knew of. I stayed with him at his Huntington Beach home and tagged along with him all day long.

At this time, finding good deals on used gym equipment was very hard. There wasn't a lot of used equipment on the market, even through the gyms. The first equipment I saw was a brand-new package of beautiful black equipment with purple cushions. It was amazing. I wanted it. I was daydreaming about how beautiful it would look in my new gym. It was perfect: twelve machines and a large jungle gym. I asked the price, and it was $40,000 for the package. That was just about all the money I had to buy the equipment for the whole gym. I had to slap myself and wake up. This wasn't even close to the amount of equipment the gym needed. I needed everything.

I was taken to a nearby warehouse where they had more equipment stored, and it was discouraging. It was all old, odd colors, and it looked mostly like old junk. Of course, the sales guy told me it was all the best of the best equipment, but the truth was, I didn't want to put this ugly crap in my new gym. I couldn't see it working.

I went out to lunch with the owner, Craig. He didn't have an answer for me. He said he could only offer me what he had in his space at the moment. When we got back to his office, we were sitting at his desk talking about options, and he said he didn't have anything else to offer. At that moment, I picked up a piece of paper that was on his desk and looked at it. It was a listing for a full gym, priced at $25,000. I thought, *That's perfect for me! I would still have about $15,000 for shipping, broker, import, and everything else.* It was a real complete gym, large, and complete with cardio.

I said, "Hey, what about this gym?" He looked at me with some confusion. I showed him the fax. He hadn't thought about this one. It was a gym he would be getting soon. I pointed out the $25,000, and he quickly corrected me. The $25,000 was his price for the whole gym, but no way he was including the cardio. He could sell that for a lot.

Within a few hours, we were on a plane to Phoenix. We saw the gym that same evening. I walked in and knew it was perfect as soon as I saw it. It was a large LA Fitness club that was still open and working. It was perfect for me and my needs. It was all white with green cushions. Those were the common colors for that period. We spent the night in the Phoenix area. The gym was an LA Fitness in Mesa, Arizona. The next morning, we were on a plane back to California, specifically, Huntington Beach. Craig was a kind of cold and ruthless, take-no-prisoners businessman. He was a skinny, white, middle-aged man with blue eyes and thinning blond hair. He smoked these strong Capone cigarettes and drank a lot.

Once we got back, we started to negotiate. He wanted all the cardio equipment. We negotiated $25,000 for everything except the cardio. I could have everything in the club, which included the TVs, refrigerators, service room stuff, all of it. I offered to save him time and money and load the cardio for him. I was kissing his ass. He was the man in the used gym equipment business. He still had to talk to his good friend and owner of the LA Fitness chain, Chin Lee. There were a few concerns and details to work out.

That afternoon, he told me it was a *go*, but there was one important detail. They were breaking the lease, and if the landlord found out, he could lock us out. We had to do it that same weekend, the Fourth of July, which was one day away. He told me I needed to first focus on getting all the equipment out of the building and into the parking lot. The landlord couldn't do anything about that. Once it was outside, he couldn't keep it or do anything.

So I now had to arrange for two trucks that would go all the way down to the Laredo border and cross into Mexico, and all the way down to GDL. I also needed a forklift and workers. There are special four-wheel floor dollies that are used to move fitness equipment, and without them, it's almost impossible. I had to bring those with me from Craig's warehouse. I returned to Arizona immediately and got to work. First, I went to the gym to make sure everything was the same and take a mental note of what I needed to do to get it out, move it, and pack it into a truck. It wasn't my first time moving gym equipment or loading it, but this was the first full club on location. It was all on me, and it wasn't like I had a system behind me or unlimited resources. I had $40,000 liquid to handle everything: that was $25,000 for the equipment and $15,000 for the two semi trucks, custom broker, and all the taxes and fees. It was a really tight budget.

I drove around the area looking for spots where migrant workers hang out waiting for work. I saw a couple of Hispanic-looking guys outside a 7-Eleven and stopped to talk to them. I started speaking Spanish to them, and one of them got really pissed off and almost attacked me.

"Yo, bro, why you speak that shit to me? I'm a native Indian, not Mexican."

I finally found five Mexicans and told them I would need them for two days. We agreed on the rate, and they jumped in my car.

The night before I left for Arizona to load the gym and after the negotiations were over and the deal was done, Craig lightened up. I spent the night at his house, and he had a buddy over for a few drinks and to smoke a cigar. I entertained them with my cigar stories, and they were all in. These guys had boring lives. They worked all day, went home at night to sleep, and then repeated it the next day. They couldn't get enough of the stories of beautiful women and wild, hot nights in Havana, Michael Jordan, and the Chicago Bears.

That night, Craig became human for a moment and treated me like a peer. We even struck a bargain. I still had thirty-plus boxes and a few bundles (*masos*) of cigars in my mother's closet back home, and we traded. I would send him some boxes, and he would trade me for treadmills and bikes. I was a good deal for both of us. The boxes were $350–$500 per box and probably worth even more in California. I sent him the boxes a few weeks later, and I waited a few more weeks to program my truck, because I had spent so much money already on the other truck and import.

When I got to the gym, I first noticed that the really cool upper-torso statue of Joe Weider was missing. I had wanted it badly, but it was gone, along with a few other obvious things. I called Craig and he told me this was normal. Once the employees find out a gym is closing, they help themselves to stuff. I really wanted it! It would have looked great in my gym; Joe Weider was a bodybuilding icon. I didn't even have keys to the club, and once I got there, all the employees left and basically abandoned the place.

I immediately organized the guys and directed them to pull everything out to the parking lot. I then told one of the guys to disassemble the equipment that wouldn't fit through the doors. Members kept coming in, and they were really affecting my focus. So, I made a sign and taped it to the front door telling them that members could go to another club. Several members weren't agreeable with going to another club, and they made a scene. One guy insisted on getting his workout even though the equipment was halfway disassembled.

To avoid a scene, I didn't pay attention to him and just worked around him. We worked until late that night and had only about half of the equipment outside. Although I loaded all the cardio for Craig and sent his trucks off to him, I was still kissing his ass even though I was the customer. I knew it would be a good investment in the future. Since I didn't have a key, and I definitely didn't want to have any problems, I decided to sleep in the gym. The air conditioning was on, and it was freezing. I used towels to sleep on and cover myself. I didn't sleep very well, but I was pumped with adrenaline about the whole ordeal. I pushed through the pain like a fuckin' Marine.

The guys were back early the next morning, and my first truck was there too. We continued to move stuff outside, and I also started loading the truck. That's when I discovered something beyond my control. The sun was so hot in Arizona that the equipment got even hotter, and we couldn't even touch it. It was burning our hands! Again, I tried my hardest to just push through it, but it was nearly impossible. It was the Fourth of July, and most stores were closed. So, I attempted to use towels, the strips of towels, and I even wet the strips to help, but they got hot, they ripped, and it was very difficult. So, I went on a mission to find an open store.

I eventually found a grocery store and got some really crappy brown cloth gloves that were better than the towels. Not only were the machines hot, but the weight plates and dumbbells were boiling!

It was miserable. Just like everything in my life, it was loaded with obstacles and challenges I needed to resolve, with no option but to figure it out.

By the end of the second day, I had everything jammed into the two trucks. It was a very hard two days' work, and I was beat. After paying the workers, I was almost out of money. I asked the trucker if I could take the ride with him all the way down to Laredo, Texas. It's a thousand miles of road and a long way from home. I was exhausted. Imagine: it had been about five days and almost no rest or sleep, not much food, and two days of grueling labor in 115-degree temperatures. He let me sleep in his bunk, and we rolled on down the road. Once we got to Laredo, I crossed the border into Mexico on foot, made my way to the bus station, and took a fifteen-hour bus ride through the mountains of Mexico to GDL.

I got home and immediately landed on the ground running. I needed to prepare all the paperwork for the import. It was up to me to make the invoices (fakes). I had to use copy machines, typewriters, and a corrector to get them to look legit. I also had a lot of work still left to finish before I could open the new area. I had walls to remove and repair, paint to be applied, and logos to create and hand-paint on the walls.

Once the equipment arrived, I had to unload it from the semi right there in the street in front of the gym. I had to lift and hoist it to the second and third floors, and I started to fix it up myself. I cleaned, sanded, painted, touched up, and did everything myself. I worked all day and into the night for a few weeks to get it done. Once I was done, it looked really good.

I had a sweet moment of gratification. It felt good. It was my gym. It was now big and complete. It was an amazing feeling.

When I started my cigar adventure, I was still a bit green and lacked some higher level of business experience and confidence. My years in the cigar business were my years of a master's degree. I met a lot of great guys from many different backgrounds. I got to rub shoulders with the top athletes from my hometown who were owners of all the cool nightclubs, restaurants, and lounges. I had the honor of smoking a cigar with all of them.

I rubbed elbows with a lot of businessmen, celebrities, and more. There were nightclub owners, lawyers, stockbrokers, and bonds traders, the owner of the largest taxi company, sports figures, baseball players, football players, basketball stars, coaches, radio personalities, sports managers, cigar store owners, trucking tycoons, pizza parlor owners, window manufacturers, restauranteurs of all types, doctors, dentists, real estate developers, luxury limousine company owners, managers of the hottest nightclubs of the moment, the creator of the most popular cigar ashtrays of the period, car salesmen, car dealership managers, photographers, cigar lounge owners, car dealership owners, health club owners, McDonald's owners, jewelers, the city's largest home-remodeling company owner, the king of the Rolex, judges, police, politicians, bankers, gangsters, and more.

I spent time with all of them. I socialized and smoked cigars with most. I can proudly state I respected all of them, and that none were robbed, burglarized, or kidnapped on my watch. None of my old habits came into play, and none of my old crew was tipped off to potential fortunes waiting to be taken.

The most important lesson was what I figured out about myself, business, and becoming rich. What I'm about to say is not meant to be negative or to offend anyone. It's not out of arrogance either. I discovered that I was as smart or smarter than almost all of them. I figured out that I could have been anything or done anything if I had only pursued it. Given different circumstances in life, I was capable of almost anything.

I learned that making money and becoming rich wasn't all about how smart you are, but more about how much pain and stress you can take, and how much time you put into the project. It's about dedication and sacrifice.

It's also about what you do with what you make. If you like to blow money, it doesn't matter how much you make; you can waste it and end up with nothing. It was an amazing adventure mixed with a first-quality education. Every time I look back on that time, I smile. I have memories almost no one else on Earth has. I've made the life I wanted for myself. And now I've finally been able to tell the story of how I got here.

THE REAL ENDING OR THE TRUE BEGINNING

The best part is…it didn't really end here.

It was a whole new beginning.

I went on to buy the master franchising rights for Gold's Gym for the entire country of Mexico. That's right. A guy who once smuggled cigars across borders now holds the rights to one of the most iconic fitness brands in the world.

I opened five massive Gold's Gyms of my own and built them from the ground up. Designed, financed, ran, and owned them outright. And then I franchised thirty-four more clubs to others. But I didn't just franchise the name; I built an entire ecosystem. Their contracts, which I put together with the help of a lawyer friend (for free), required them to buy their equipment, supplements, apparel, souvenirs, and everything from my company. I had created my own fitness empire.

Three of my gyms were the hottest spots in town. Status symbols. Celebrities, athletes, models, and everybody wanted to be seen at Gold's.

At the height of it all, I had a real office with a full-time staff, sales teams, receptionists, accountants, and even an in-house lawyer. I had graphic designers, a marketing director, and a small media team. I was also publishing and distributing the Spanish-language version of a major US bodybuilding magazine with distribution throughout the Spanish-speaking world.

Then I started importing fitness equipment by the truckload. I built a business out of it. Hell, I built a 100,000-square-foot warehouse and became the largest distributor of fitness equipment in all of Mexico.

At my peak, I had over three hundred employees. Three hundred people who looked to me for leadership. Me, the kid who once ran the streets and dodged prison like it was a sport. Now I was the boss of multiple businesses, running meetings, making deals, and cutting checks. I had done it. I had become what I once only hoped I could be: a respected man and a real member of society.

I remember one Christmas when we rented out an entire restaurant for our company party. The place was packed with my employees, their families, and their laughter. I sat there at the head table with a drink in hand, watching it all. For a moment, I went quiet. I just looked around and thought, *Look what I built.*

I had made it out of the chaos, out of the streets, out of the system, and into a life I never imagined would get this big. And here's the thing: I was ready for it. It didn't come too soon. It didn't fall into my lap. By the time I reached that point, I had earned it. And I wasn't about to throw it away.

I never looked back.

I stopped breaking the law. I learned to control my impulses. I stayed away from people who weren't living right. Sure, I still knew some of them, and now and then we'd sit down, tell stories, and laugh about the old days. But I was on a different path now.

Most days, I was up before the sun and didn't stop moving until it went down. I loved what I was doing. I was building something for myself and for my family. I wasn't chasing fast money anymore. I had dedicated myself to a mission. And I made it.

No formal training. No roadmap. No mentors. No handouts.

Just me—raw, relentless, and finally free.

Somehow, I broke through that ceiling. I didn't just make it out, I went places, saw things, and lived a life that would've sounded like a fantasy to the kid I used to be. **And for better or worse, I did it my way.**

When I look back now, I realize I didn't just survive the life I was given. I rewrote it.

Lately, I've been reflecting on my life and everything that's happened, where I came from, and where I am today. I am one of the only people still standing from where I came from. There are a few souls still alive, but they're just surviving, not thriving.

The old neighborhood didn't produce the kind of guy I sell cigars to in this story; it produced blue-collar guys.

I recently had breakfast with an older friend of mine, a retired stockbroker and Notre Dame graduate. During the course of our conversation, we were discussing our roots. To gain some perspective and to illustrate the point I was trying to make, I asked him a series of questions.

Have you ever been arrested?

Have you ever gone to jail or prison?

Has anyone ever pointed a gun at you?

Have you ever pointed a gun at someone?

Have you ever seen someone being killed in front of you?
Have you ever known anyone who went to prison?
Do you know anyone who's still in prison?
Have you ever known anyone who was murdered?
Have you ever known anyone who committed murder?
His answers were always the same: "No. None. No. None."
Mine were all the same too: "Yes."

Where and how I grew up was beyond my control. It wasn't even destiny. I was just one of those anonymous thugs who ran the streets just like thousands of others who run the streets of every shithole city in America. I was nothing special. Quite the opposite, actually.

CLOSING NOTE

This book tells the story of my years as a Cuban cigar smuggler—a journey of danger, excitement, sacrifice, transformation, and redemption. What you've read here is only part of the story. I made over sixty trips to Havana, more than I could ever recount in one book. There were too many adventures, too many women, too many friends and enemies, too many nights of risk and smoke to capture them all. I've chosen the best—the ones that shaped me, tested me, and nearly broke me—to share with you. My goal was not to list every trip, but to let you feel the ride, the struggle, the thrill, and the transformation.

Yes, smuggling cigars was a crime. I was breaking federal laws, dodging ATF regulations, and violating the Trading with the Enemy Act. But I refused to return to serious crime: drugs, guns, violence, and the kind of life that destroys men. Instead, I built myself back with willpower, intelligence, and sheer determination. It was hard, it was dangerous, but it was also the ride of a lifetime. And now, I've shared that ride with you.

ACKNOWLEDGMENTS

BEFORE THE CIGARS, THERE WERE THE ANGELS. I DIDN'T KNOW it at the time, but they were sent to me by God, Jesus, a saint, an angel, or some force bigger than anything I could understand. They crossed my path exactly when I needed them, and each one, in their own way, saved me.

Mike Lindenmayer was one of the first, maybe the first. He helped me when nobody else did. Then came Kathi, the school psychologist, who was the single biggest influence in my life. Without her, I wouldn't be who I am today. Andy from Oak School was probably the most influential male figure in my life. He showed me, without even knowing it, what a real man was. Randy Bramlet was sent to guide and protect me. Leno Morfin rescued me from myself at a desperate moment and unknowingly set me on the path destiny had waiting for me. And Georgia attorney Thomas Garwood, sent by God at one of the most pivotal moments of my life, went far beyond his duty to help me.

Without them, I never would have made it to the point in my life where the cigar story even begins.

During the cigar years, there were others. Antonio had my back all the way. Eduardo, without him, the struggle would have been much harder. Even Oscar, who was with me in the trenches.

Howard Frum, the Chicago Rolex King, whose generosity made it all possible. He trusted me, had faith in me, and introduced me to so many people. He opened every door I needed to walk through. Without Howard, this business never would have happened.

The late Gary Kron, who adopted me like a son, let me lean on him through it all, treated me like family, and made the road easier.

Shaun Gayle and Richard Dent, both Chicago Bears legends, were friends who welcomed me into their lives, introduced me to countless people, and opened their homes. Always gracious, always generous.

And to every customer I ever had, thank you. Without you, none of this would have been possible.

SCAN TO ENTER THE WORLD OF SCOTT ANTHONY OG

- All social media links in one place
- Bonus stories, podcasts, and unreleased chapters
- High-resolution photo archives from the events, trips, and operations described in *Smoke: Confessions of a Cuban Cigar Smuggler*

Visit: www.ScottAnthonyOG.com

Full galleries and exclusive content

ABOUT THE AUTHOR

SCOTT ANTHONY built an underground empire smuggling Cuban cigars, making over sixty trips to Havana and moving millions in black-market contraband. Raised on Chicago's streets, he rose from troubled youth to gang leader, learning survival the hard way in a world of danger and betrayal. His life became a gamble—border crossings, payoffs, and moves that could cost everything. After years as a fugitive, Scott rebuilt in Mexico, opening gyms, managing world-class fighters, and running businesses with hundreds of employees. A boxer, kickboxer, lifelong martial artist, and student of jujitsu, he's now telling his story.

www.ingramcontent.com/pod-product-compliance
Lightning Source LLC
Chambersburg PA
CBHW030515080526
44586CB00011B/202